Reading Theologically

Foundations for Learning

Eric D. Barreto

Fortress Press
Minneapolis

READING THEOLOGICALLY

Foundations for Learning

Cover image: Antishock/123RF

Cover design: Laurie Ingram

Library of Congress Cataloging-in-Publication Data

Print ISBN: 978-1-4514-8342-0

eBook ISBN: 978-1-4514-8752-7

The paper used in this publication meets the minimum requirements of American National Standard for Information Sciences — Permanence of Paper for Printed Library Materials, ANSI Z329.48-1984.

Manufactured in the U.S.A.

This book was produced using PressBooks.com, and PDF rendering was done by PrinceXML.

Reading Theologically

Contents

Contributors

Melissa Browning is an assistant professor at Loyola University Chicago's Institute of Pastoral Studies. She is the author of *Risky Marriage: HIV and Intimate Relationships in Tanzania* (2013).

Gerald C. Liu is assistant professor of Homiletics and Worship Arts at Drew Theological School. He is the author of book chapters and articles concerning Asian American preaching and worship and the interplay between theology and music.

James W. McCarty III received his Ph.D. in Religion, Ethics, and Society from Emory University. He has published peer-reviewed articles in the *Journal of the Society of Christian Ethics, Theology and Sexuality, St. John's Law Review,* and *West Virginia Law Review*.

Sarah Morice-Brubaker is assistant professor of Theology at Phillips Theological Seminary. She is the author of *The Place of the Spirit: Toward a Trinitarian Theology of Location* (2013).

Jacob D. Myers recently completed his Ph.D. at Emory University in homiletics. He has published articles on theology and sexuality, poststructural philosophy, and alternative epistemologies for preaching and worship. He is also co-managing editor for Practical Matters (http://www.practicalmattersjournal.org/).

Amy L. B. Peeler is assistant professor of New Testament at Wheaton College. She is a postulant for the priesthood with the Episcopal Church, USA. She is the author of *"You Are My Son": The Family of God in the Epistle to the Hebrews* (2014).

Miriam Y. Perkins is associate professor of Theology & Society at Emmanuel Christian Seminary. She is the author of several interdisciplinary articles in theology.

Shanell T. Smith is assistant professor of New Testament and Christian Origins at Hartford Seminary. She is the author of the forthcoming *The Woman Babylon and the Marks of Empire: Reading Revelation with a Postcolonial Womanist Hermeneutics of Ambiveilence* (Fortress).

Introduction

Eric D. Barreto

Reading is so commonplace that we often don't even notice how much of it we do. When we think about reading, we might imagine curling up with a novel next to a roaring fire on a cold winter's night or hunkering down in a library for research. We might picture delighting in a graphic novel on an iPad or a glossy magazine full of advice for better living. Or we might recall the more mundane forms of reading we encounter every day: bills, reports, road signs.

And yet reading extends beyond deciphering marks on a page. We "read" the outdoors, finding there a weather forecast or inspiration. We "read" social situations and discover joy or apprehension. We "read" our friends and family and discern without words their emotional state. In short, reading is a habit as much as it is a practice, a way of life as much as it is an academic skill.

As you ponder your own theological education, reading theologically seems a particularly appropriate starting point. As you embark on this educational journey, you will read books and essays in preparation for the work of ministry. You will read the Bible, histories, theological reflections, pastoral care resources. But you will also be walking through this experience with fellow students and faculty who will have much to teach you.

Some of what you will read will delight you, confirm your deepest hopes, drive you to new aspirations, and perhaps even help you encounter God in powerful ways. At other times, you will read texts and encounter ideas that will disturb you, shake you to your core, lead you to question and doubt much of what you have held dear. Both are indispensable experiences of reading in seminary. Both are necessary. Both will challenge you. Both will be difficult. Yet the moments when reading challenges us—whether by delighting or disturbing us—are precisely the moments when we make our greatest strides in learning.

How to Read This Book

This book is a collaboration of eight theologically-minded scholar-teachers. All eight are exemplary scholars in their particular fields and incisive theologians. Moreover, all are deeply committed to the kind of formative and graceful reading I have been describing, even as we might disagree on a number of issues. In these eight distinct perspectives, you will thus discover a set of shared values about reading theologically. In the ensuing chapters, we emphasize the vital skills, practices, and values involved in reading theologically. However, this is not just a "how-to" book or an instruction manual for how to read. Indeed, you already know quite well how to read. After all, you have been reading these several paragraphs thanks to a lifetime of reading! Instead, we are more concerned with helping you inculcate a particular set of habits around reading that will serve you well in all kinds of ministry settings. What posture do you take toward those with whom you disagree? How can reading widen your perspective rather than just confirm what you think you know? How can reading transform your spirituality?

Reading is not just an activity of the eyes and the brain. What we mean by reading theologically is a whole mindset and posture toward texts and ideas, people and communities alike. Reading theologically is thus not primarily about mechanics. This book is not principally concerned with *how* we read in seminary. Instead, reading theologically is about the formation and cultivation of a particular posture toward texts, whether sacred or profane. Reading theologically is not just about building your academic skills, but about your formation as a ministerial leader who can engage scholarship critically, interpret scripture and tradition faithfully, welcome different perspectives, and help lead others to do the same. This is your call as a student of theology.

Each contribution in this book will include practical advice about best practices in reading theologically; however, we will also stress why particular reading postures and attitudes are essential for those called to ministry. The essays in this book will invite you to read in many different ways. Each assumes that you, the reader, are considering attending seminary or have already begun your theological education. However, no matter where you are in your discernment, this book will help you think about this critical habit of a lifelong learner. In short, this book will invite you to be a perpetual pupil, a student always unsatisfied with easy answers for difficult questions or simple caricatures of those with whom you disagree.

Why is reading theologically so important? Because the gospel of Jesus Christ demands a radical posture of grace toward ideas and people alike. With a spirit of generosity, we expect God to speak in all kinds of ways through all kinds of people. With conviction and passion we draw upon the scriptures, our traditions, and our experiences, knowing that God meets us in the everyday sacredness of life. Reading is never just about the collection of data; it is always about the cultivation of a deep wisdom rooted in the Spirit's gracious shaping of our lives.

An Exhortation to the Reader

Let's face it, your education and formation in seminary is not really about books and articles, curricula and programs, tests and essays. Your education is not about stuffing a ton of information in between your ears and being prepared to parrot it back to your teachers. Your education is not about confirming everything you know or rejecting everything you believe. Your education will not just happen in the classroom or in the library.

After all, why are you in seminary? You are pursuing this particular form of education because you were and are called. Right? You are drawn to seminary because God brought family, friends, and mentors into your life who helped kindle your gifts and passions. You are considering theological education because God has called you to serve the world, to preach the good news, to heal the sick, to declare the reign of God's justice. You are in seminary because your classmates need you so that they too might serve the world. You are in seminary because an increasingly diverse world yearns for a word of hope, a violent world yearns for peace, an unjust world yearns for a new king.

So, are you ready?

If you consider the requisite qualifications of a seminarian to be a vast amount of prior knowledge, you are not ready. If you consider the requisite qualifications of a seminarian to be certainty and assurance about all things, you are not ready. If you consider the requisite qualifications of a seminarian to be a desire to surpass all others in argumentation, you are not ready.

But if you lean on God's call when the work piles up, you are ready. If you learn with a generous heart and listen to your colleagues with genuine curiosity, you are ready. If love is your guide when you read and write and discuss and think and debate, you are ready. And, most importantly, if God has called you to this path, you are ready.

So, are you ready? You are, my friends. You are. Let's get to work. Let's read . . . together.

1

Reading Basically

Melissa Browning

(Re)learning to Read

I was a junior in college when I first learned to read—really read—at an academic level. I was taking an upper-level New Testament course and, after several dismal presentations by students in the course, the professor decided we had never really learned to read. He told us that when you read an academic text or when you read Scripture it should involve more than just reading (and, one hopes, comprehending) words. You must dialogue with the text, he said. He advised that when you read Scripture for an academic class you should read it again and again. Then, when you think you understand it, when you've dialogued with the text, that's when you should set a circle of chairs and invite the scholars you are reading to join your conversation.[1]

---

1. I'm grateful to Dr. R. Wayne Stacey for teaching me this lesson while he was my professor at Gardner-Webb University.

In that moment, I latched onto that image. I pictured myself sitting on a barstool having a conversation with the scholars assigned on the syllabus. This visual metaphor taught me to read in a different way. Books were no longer a collection of words on a page that were "interesting" or "uninteresting." They became spaces of invitation, sacred spaces to think and ponder and dialogue with a world of ideas. When my students are reading a set of academic texts, I often ask them to "set a table" as they're preparing for class. I tell them to pretend they're having a dinner party and the authors we've been reading are coming to dinner. I ask them to imagine asking these thinkers questions or putting them in dialogue with each other on a current issue. And in doing so, I ask them to (re)learn to read as they remember that words printed on a page are meant to be a conversation we are invited to engage rather than a set of facts we need to memorize.

Graduate school is a time when you learn to read all over again. This period of your life requires a new literacy, a new way of being with texts that does not forget the people who surround you. If you've ever helped a child learn to read, you know that becoming literate takes practice. I have a two-year-old who is deeply interested in letters and words. When she looks through her books, she tells us she's "reading." But when she picks up one of our books off the shelf (with no pictures and so many words), she says, "Look Mom, it's ABCs!"

For my two-year-old, the letters have not yet begun to take shape and leap off the page as words and then sentences that have meaning. Whether you're a student or a lifelong learner, reading is always a *practice* we cultivate. Reading is not only a place to listen to texts or explore theory but also a place to connect what we are reading to our communities of accountability.

Reading as Practice

As a teacher, I am in the classroom with a brilliant group of graduate students who are activists, organizers, and educators, most of whom work in the non-profit world. They did not come to graduate school to explore the life of the mind, but to learn how to create social change more effectively. Naturally, the most common complaint I hear in the classroom is "this is just theory. It is not practical." At these points in our teaching and learning together, I attempt to connect the two as I argue that good theory (though not all theory) can shape our practices.

This is an important distinction, for reading is not something we do only with our "minds." In Western cultures, we live with the legacy of the mind/body split, where the mind was seen as greater than and separate from the body. The lingering effects of this philosophy shape our educational systems as we talk about a "life of the mind" as if it could be separate from our embodied reality and relationalities. Learning to (re)read means a commitment to stepping away from the legacy of a mind/body dualism and reading in a way that cares for ourselves and our communities, reading in a way that opens space for both action and reflection. In order to do this, we must learn to read in a way that is embodied, communal, spiritual, and transformative in practice.

Reading as an Embodied Practice

Unfortunately, higher education can make a convincing argument for mind/body dualism when students learn to value their minds and ignore their bodies. Think of the times when you've stayed up late reading, crammed for a test that is due the next day, or "pulled an all-nighter" writing that final paper. In these times, the body's need to sleep or pause for a healthy meal is often neglected. During one semester in graduate school, I ate dinner out of a vending machine every Monday night because I taught an afternoon class and was taking an evening class. Each week I swore to myself that I would pack healthy food to bring with me, but an entire semester passed without my ever remembering to do so. I was giving priority to my mind without paying attention to the needs of my body, and in doing so I was creating a division that was unhealthy for mind and body alike.

Believing in and practicing a mind/body dualism is a particular danger of graduate school that is often experienced when we sit down to read. We do not often think of reading as an embodied practice, but in truth we read with our bodies as much as we read with our minds. Too often, when reading, we wage a war on our bodies—forcing ourselves to concentrate, to ignore distractions, to commit the words on the page to memory. I would suggest that the first task in (re)learning to read is learning how to read as embodied people.

In talking about embodiment, Margaret Farley says that we are "embodied spirits" and "inspirited bodies."[2] As we recognize this truth about ourselves, we also recognize how we are vulnerable to the world and experience life in ways that are often more fragmented than we would like. In other words, we rarely live fully into who we mean to be. Recognizing this vulnerability allows us to be patient with ourselves as we (re)learn to read. Getting distracted does not mean that you lack intelligence or that the person you are reading is more intelligent than you. Getting distracted simply means you are an embodied being, a person who grows weary and can be bored. You are not a machine that you can command at will.

2. Margaret Farley, *Just Love: A Framework for Christian Sexual Ethics* (New York: Continuum, 2006), 116–18.

Reading with our bodies means, first, learning to pay attention to what our bodies need: rest, relaxation, food that does not come from a vending machine. These things are important. But reading with our bodies also means reading in the midst of our lived experiences. It means listening to the rhythms and memories of our own bodies as we read the text. For example, it is possible to read about a subject such as baptism without ever connecting the words we read with our own experiences. But when we read as "embodied spirits" and "inspirited bodies," this same text might connect with us in a way that allows us to feel the waters of our own baptisms again. This allows us to dialogue with the text in a way that is both material and embodied as we put what we read in dialogue with our own lives and the lived experiences of others.

Reading as a Communal Practice

Reading is not only an embodied practice but also a communal practice. When we come to a text, we not only bring our own lived experiences but also the lived experiences of our communities. One important lesson I learned in graduate school is that all of our reading, writing, and study are worth little if we do it without a community of accountability.[3]

Let me give an illustration.

In East Africa, when a young person from a poor community is accepted to a university, the community will often throw a *harambee* to raise the money for the student's tuition. The Kiswahili word *harambee* means "pull together," and the idea behind this event is that the community not only helps the student but also makes an

---

3. I'm grateful to my professor and colleague, Aana Marie Vigen, for teaching me this lesson.

investment as the student is expected to return home with her or his new knowledge and help the community.

While most of you will not receive a *harambee* before starting your theological education, you still come to seminary bound to communities of accountability, groups of people who are counting on you to succeed. These may be your families, your churches, or people in specific groups who are marginalized or oppressed. These communities of accountability are important because they give meaning to your work. They remind you that you study not only for your own fulfillment but also to contribute to the common good.

One of my primary communities of accountability is a group of women living with HIV and AIDS in Mwanza, Tanzania, who are collaborators in my research.[4] When I read and write, I know that I am accountable to them because they have trusted me with their stories. When I was writing about our work together, I kept a picture of these women on my desk to remind me of the commitment I made to write a book that shared their stories. Likewise, before I worked with this community in Mwanza, I spent more than two years reading literature on the African AIDS pandemic. After I had worked with these women, the literature took on new meanings as I listened to texts with their stories in mind.

During my research in Mwanza, one memorable part of the focus group sessions I conducted was "reading" certain theological texts with the women. While there was a language barrier because these texts were not published in Kiswahili, I summarized key theological concepts and theories I planned to use in the book I was writing and asked them their opinion on the authors' ideas. In one session we talked about John Rawls's original position and the veil of ignorance,[5]

---

4. Melissa Browning, *Risky Marriage: HIV and Intimate Relationships in Tanzania* (Lanham, MD: Lexington Books, 2013).
5. John Rawls, "Justice as Fairness," *The Philosophical Review* 67/2 (1958): 164–94.

and I asked them to use this concept to create rules and guidelines for an "ideal village." In other sessions, I took the stories of the women and put them in dialogue with writings from the Circle of Concerned African Women Theologians. These were some of my favorite sessions, as I listened to the women talk about these theologians as "this mama" or "that mama" when they gave their opinions on the texts, thus identifying with the theologians in relational ways that are not common in Western theological speech.

Reading is a communal practice not only because we come from communities and read in the midst of our communities, but also because books (or good books, at least) are written in community. In my focus groups in Mwanza, the women deeply identified with the work of Mercy Oduyoye, Musa Dube, and others more than they resonated with the work of John Rawls because Oduyoye and Dube were speaking from their communities of accountability, and those communities were ones that resembled the group of women assembled in Mwanza.[6]

When we recognize reading as a communal practice, we learn to pull up a circle of chairs, not only for other scholars whom we ask to join the dialogue but also for folks from our community whose lived experiences matter to our work.

6. Some particular texts we used for this exercise were Musa Dube, "Adinkra! Four Hearts Joined Together," 131–56 in *African Women, Religion, And Health: Essays In Honor Of Mercy Amba Ewudzi Oduyoye*, ed. Isabel Apawo Phiri, Sarojini Nadar, and Mercy Amba Oduyoye (Maryknoll, NY: Orbis Books, 2006); Mercy Amba Oduyoye, "A Coming Home to Myself: The Childless Woman in the West African Space," 105–20 in *Liberating Eschatology: Essays in Honor of Letty Russell*, ed. Margaret A. Farley and Serene Jones (Louisville: Westminster John Knox, 1999); idem., "Be a Woman and Africa Will Be Strong," 35–53 in *Inheriting our Mothers' Gardens: Feminist Theology in Third World Perspective,* ed. Letty Russell et. al. (Philadelphia: Westminster Press, 1988).

Reading as a Spiritual Practice

Reading is not only an embodied and communal practice; it is also a spiritual practice. It is tied to our vocation as ministers and as people of God. Reading can help us discern or refine God's call on our lives. Reading should not be the hoop we jump through to pass the class to get a piece of paper that gives us credentials to be a minister.

In other words, we should not see reading or study as a means to an end but as an end in itself. (Re)learning to read is a practice we refine because we care for our communities, our calls, and our God.

For instance, when writing on worship Marva Dawn talks about the importance of giving our best work to God as we plan a worship service and argues that this best work is necessary because our planning is a gift we bring to God.[7] Your work as you study theology in this time and this place is part of your vocation as a minister, as a person belonging to God. For this reason, let your reading be part of your spiritual practice. This might be easier in some places than others, for instance when reading scripture or inspirational writings. In other readings, our spiritual practice is less about being caught up in the inspiration and more about living out our call through diligence in our work.

Helmut Thielicke wrote a wonderful book called *A Little Exercise for Young Theologians* that is an excellent read for students of theology.[8] In this book, Thielicke builds on Anselm to say: "A theological thought can breathe only in the atmosphere of dialogue with God."[9] Thielicke warns theology students that they should not become so accustomed to reading scripture with an eye to exegesis

---

7. Marva J. Dawn, *Reaching out Without Dumbing Down: A Theology of Worship for the Turn-of-the-Century Culture* (Grand Rapids: Eerdmans, 1995).
8. Helmut Thielicke, *A Little Exercise for Young Theologians*, trans. Charles L. Taylor (Grand Rapids: Eerdmans, 1961).
9. Ibid., 34.

that they are no longer able to hear how scripture might "speak" to their lives. Extending Thielicke's argument, I think this maxim applies not only to scripture but to other things we read as well. Reading as a spiritual practice is not only a way to give our best gifts to God but is also a way of learning to listen for God's voice in the most unexpected places.

Reading as a Transformative Practice

In (re)learning to read, it is important to begin by questioning why we are reading. Do we read to memorize content, or perhaps to be transformed?

Brazilian educator Paulo Freire forever changed the way many people think about education by tying it to liberation. Freire argued that education usually employs a "banking model" in which students memorize content and then give it back to their teacher. In this model, the teacher is the source of all understanding, while the students are meant solely to reflect this understanding back to the teacher. An example of this type of learning might be the "teach to the test" paradigm in which teachers spend their time preparing students for standardized tests. Freire instead argues for a "problem-posing" model of education that leads to what he calls "conscientization." In this way of learning, teachers are not the sole source of knowledge in the classroom, but instead are collaborators with students in creating a critical consciousness that allows learners to become agents of their own liberation.[10]

When we think about reading and the way we normally approach a text to prepare for a class or an exam, we must admit that the banking model is often at play. It is deeply important that we

10. Paulo Freire, *Pedagogy of the Oppressed* (New York: Continuum, 1997).

comprehend a text, and sometimes we even need to memorize content, but this does not mean that we have to practice a banking system of education. Our commitment to our own conscientization, to our own liberation and the liberation of others, can allow us to read in ways that create space for transformation. Reading for conscientization requires a deep engagement with the text that does not neglect the embodied, communal, and spiritual aspects of reading.

Within the field of higher education there is the idea that once a student understands a "threshold concept," his or her perception of the subject of study can be transformed. For me, the idea of conscientization as opposed to a banking system of education has been a "threshold concept" that has changed the way I read, write, teach, and learn. The beauty and the privilege of being in graduate school is that you have set aside space to chase ideas, explore theories, and learn in the midst of a still-busy life. Yet I have never met a graduate student who felt they had enough time to do all these things. Life is always busy. There are always commitments outside of graduate work.

However, reading with an eye toward transformation allows us to bring our whole selves and our whole communities to the work we do. It allows us to read and learn as a spiritual practice whereby we honor God with our work and discern our own vocations. Once we move away from the banking system of education and reading, we are better able to live an integrated life in which graduate-school coursework builds on the realities and vocations of our lives.

The Privilege of Reading:
Deconstructing and Reconstructing with Texts

The classroom, particularly the graduate school classroom, is a space of privilege. It is an exclusive space primarily for those who have the credentials, time, money, and resources to become students. But while other forms of privilege (such as white privilege or economic privilege) are often obstacles to learning, educational privilege can provide a sacred opportunity and obligation to dismantle other privileges, if we allow it to do so.

In her book, *Teaching to Transgress,* bell hooks argues that "the classroom remains the most radical space of possibility in the academy."[11] As students, we are not only reading for our own learning but also to contribute to the learning of a community of possibility. Classrooms where we discuss texts are radical spaces of possibilities, as hooks suggests. In these spaces, the discussions that transpire can open new space for the kin-dom of God to flourish.

Books, like classrooms, are powerful sites of privilege in that those who have the credentials, ability, time, and resources to write do not represent all the voices in the kin-dom of God. For this reason, as we read we must deconstruct with a vision of reconstructing. We must ask what voices are missing or marginalized, whose stories are overlooked. Reading toward conscientization means we ask difficult questions of those we invite to sit in our circle of chairs, for we are learning not only to read but to talk back to the text and challenge its claims. This is part of living our own vocation as people committed to God's kin-dom come.

As we think about the practice of reading, we must admit that not all texts bring us inspiration or joy. Some texts we are required to read are terribly dull; others are badly written. (Re)learning to read

11. bell hooks, *Teaching to Transgress: Education as the Practice of Freedom* (New York: Routledge, 1994), 11.

academically means that we engage texts by looking for what they have to teach us (particularly if they are required readings for our coursework!). But is also means we read with a critical eye as we critique a text's weaknesses and shortcomings. Sometimes the most expansive spaces of learning come from reading terrible books with which we disagree. By reading these books, we develop our own voices as we deconstruct the text.

The Practical Work of Reading

Throughout this chapter, we have explored reading basically by talking about ways to engage texts that treat reading as an embodied, communal, spiritual, and transformative practice. But what might such reading look like in practice?

First, when you read it is important to listen to the rhythms of your embodied self. There are probably times of the day when you have more energy for reading than others. Pay attention to this and reserve the times when you are most attentive for your reading. Sometimes reserving these times is difficult, but it is important for you to guard this time as sacred. Ask others to hold you accountable to keeping this time. For some people, this might mean turning off email or silencing a phone. For others, setting a timer might help to focus. One trick for doing this is the "pomodoro technique" in which you set a timer and read as much as you can until the timer goes off, then give yourself a five-minute break.[12] Very few people are good at reading large amounts at one time, particularly when the reading is dense. For this reason, it is normally better to schedule a little time each day rather than trying to read everything for class in one sitting.

12. For more on this idea see http://pomodorotechnique.com/.

Second, some people can read with distractions, while other people need a quiet environment. If you are the type of person who can take a book with you and read on the train or in short spurts here and there, then it's a great practice to keep a textbook in your bag. During my graduate studies, I would go through the syllabus and create a post-it note for each textbook. On that note I would write down each reading assignment and the date it was due. With these post-it notes in the front of each book I was able to take a textbook with me without needing to refer back to the syllabus to see what was due that week. For some people who are distracted easily when reading, it can help to have a reading playlist with instrumental music that helps you tune out distractions.

Third, certain texts are easier to read than others. For this reason, it is helpful to have a few strategies to draw on when you inevitably get stuck. One way of doing this is to read a book review on the text before reading the book. For most academic books, there are reviews published in academic journals that will highlight the main arguments within the book. Book abstracts and journal or chapter abstracts can also be helpful in this way.

Fourth, another way of approaching a difficult text is to skim the book before reading it. In this strategy, you begin by reading the introduction (or the first few paragraphs) and then read the headings in the chapter and think about the progression of the argument. Then read the conclusion of the book or chapter. This strategy is not a replacement for reading, but is a way to preview the text for greater retention when you read more slowly and deeply. It is also a great way of skimming a text that you think might be relevant to a research paper you are working on. Another modification of this same strategy is to read the first and last sentence of each section or the first sentence of each paragraph as a way of previewing a chapter or article.[13]

A final strategy for understanding the trajectory of a text before you begin reading is to look closely at the introduction, particularly where the author outlines what she or he will argue in each chapter. Sometimes these introductions are not part of the assigned reading but are helpful in that they allow you to see the overall arc of the book and understand better the section that is assigned.

As you read, it is also important to think about the goal of your reading. If you are reading for a paper you're writing, it is helpful to keep a running notebook of the quotations you plan to use and pages you need to reference. I sometimes do this by keeping a laptop close by and writing up what I'm reading as a paragraph I will later insert into my finished paper. When reading a text you will discuss in class, it is sometimes most helpful to take notes in a book or to use large post-it notes to write questions on the page or tabs for pages you want to reference in class. I often will use two large post-it notes for each chapter and write a chapter outline on one and my list of questions on the other. If the book is one that belongs to you, leaving these notes in the book will help you remember what you read later. It will also help as you discuss or write about the text to have a ready reference.

(Re)learning to Read Basically

As we think about what it means to "read basically," it is helpful to ask the question, "why am I reading?" or even more directly, "why am I studying at all?" A graduate degree should be more than a credential or a line on your resume. Your studies should transform you. They should inspire you to live out your calling and equip you to be a witness to God's transforming of the world. But this type of learning

---

13. I am grateful to my colleague David Creech for sharing this method with me.

requires more than showing up. It demands an active commitment on the part of the learner to be transformed.

When children first learn to read, the process is rarely easy. They become frustrated when they find words they can't pronounce, and sometimes they would rather give up and watch a story on TV rather than read it in a book. Think of your own experience trying to learn another language, perhaps in the Greek or Hebrew class your seminary requires. Becoming a reader is difficult work that takes practice.

(Re)learning to read is no different. It demands an engagement and commitment akin to the discipline required to learn a new language. Yet your newfound literacy promises great rewards as it offers you a chance to chance to engage with God and others and listen to your own life in ways that might help transform the world.

2

Reading Meaningfully

Miriam Y. Perkins

Meaningful understanding, often called "interpretation" in academic contexts, is vital throughout seminary education. Interpretation is deliberative exploration and creative expression of fruitful encounter. It is essential to understanding scripture texts, historical sources and artifacts, theological writers across time, and real-time conversations about ethical, spiritual, and pastoral matters. The finding and sharing of insight involved in interpretation is always shaped by encounters between ourselves and what we read, ourselves and other people, and our own life experiences and the presence of God.

Even so, while in seminary we rarely stop to think about the process of interpretation, the patterns of how a person reads and moves toward understanding, and how this shapes the vocational calling of ministry. In this chapter, I offer tools and strategies to enhance your ability to read meaningfully across the many kinds of texts that inform graduate seminary education. I hope you are empowered to embrace challenging reading in order to become a lifelong learner able to listen with empathy, follow the Spirit's leading, and discern, craft, and communicate redemptive truths about our relationship with God and one another.[1]

When interpretation is studied as a method, theory, or process of coming to understanding, it is categorized as the academic field of hermeneutics. Few seminary programs include an introductory course in hermeneutics and instead tend to teach interpretation as a set of methods related to biblical study. Although not always made transparent to students, differing hermeneutical commitments shape the way theological scholars approach their fields, research, and courses. Some of the disorientation you are likely to feel in seminary education, especially when compared to undergraduate education or other fields of graduate study, will result from tensions you intuit between various approaches to interpretation. For instance, one of your professors might stress a uniquely nonviolent God in the creation accounts while another dwells on a cosmically powerful God shaped by other ancient creation stories. How do you as a student negotiate these differing perspectives? Knowing that such questions are an important part of your education and having a basic orientation to the art and process of meaning-making can give you a considerable edge in pursuing seminary study.

There are two fundamental missteps to avoid in reading for theological meaning. The first is to imagine that theological insight is accessible only to insiders either with certain degree credentials, Christian status, or privileged personal/social/racial backgrounds. Seminary education can give this false impression, but theological meaning is connected to broad processes of human understanding that all people exercise and use every day in a multitude of ways

1. For their gracious insights and constructive feedback, I am grateful to Dr. Rollin A. Ramsaran, Dr. Melinda McGarrah Sharp, Rev. Keith Katterheinrich, and seminarians Conner Hall, Carly Hedrick, Thomas Ryden, and Brandon Waite.

(sometimes called "general hermeneutics"). The second misstep is to imagine that theological meaning and reading meaningfully involve no special skills, honed practices, or character formation (sometimes called "special hermeneutics"). This also is not true; seminary education involves *distinctive formation* for meaningful theological reading and interpretation.

Theological education is therefore the development of both broad and specialized literacies. It involves a whole person living into practices of discerning God's voice across unique scriptures, artifacts, artistic expressions, and social historical moments up to the present time. Meaningful understanding is Spirit-filled discernment of the overlapping dimensions of a text's history, literary artfulness, and vision of the future as they interact with your own unique standpoint informed by your life experiences. Theological literacy is essential for pastoral vocations because it involves practiced skills in theological meaning-making that have ethical consequences for how a person lives out Christian faith. This chapter is about those skills.

Meaning Is Multidimensional, Not One-dimensional

The first book I typically assign in a theology course is a novel. Starting with a novel reminds seminary students that *they already know how to read*. Much reading in seminary education is so technically, ethically, and conceptually challenging that it is easy to forget the many good skills you already have at your disposal for reading meaningfully. For example, novelists do not typically tell readers in advance who all the characters are, how the story is designed to unfold, what themes are important, or why anyone should care in the first place. A novelist has to trust readers' intuitive skills to integrate interspersed clues about characters, plot, and themes. Unless readers also trust that the process of reading will gradually build meaning and intrigue, we are inclined to put down a novel too soon. The reward comes in carrying the experience to the end and seeing the intersections of details we noticed along the way.

Novelists create complex webs of intersecting and multidimensional story components that help readers imagine and picture the world in a unique way, so that we can contemplate and respond to this world representation with feeling, insight, and/ or critique.[2] In novels, reading meaningfully includes recognizing specific features and details such as characterization, plot development, timing, symbols and themes (or their absence), and the way these elements intersect and interact over the span of a story. Reading theological texts meaningfully begins by making these intuitive reading skills we already possess more explicit and focused.

Theological writers create similar webs of meaning and analogously trust readers' intuitive skills with the tasks of navigating these webs. Bringing the elements of novels to theological interpretation can therefore be a useful starting point for interpretation. As you read assignments, begin by identifying important major and minor characters (living, dead, or imagined) or characters noticeably absent. Consider how the components of a story or essay link together sequentially as a plot. Look for clues about how a theological author privileges certain perspectives on time, whether past, present, or future. Stay attuned to narrative symbols that summarize and layer meanings in theological writing.[3] Finally,

2. Anthropologist Clifford Geertz believed cultures, including religious beliefs and practices within cultures, create "webs of significance." I use "webs" without appropriating Geertz's comprehensive perspective or its limitations. See Clifford Geertz, *The Interpretation of Cultures: Selected Essays* (New York: Basic Books, 1973), 5, 88–125.

3. For instance, when Mark describes Jesus breaking bread and saying "This is my body," he layers multiple and contrasting meanings of life and death on the image and symbol of bread with resonances to Passover and the miracle of loaves and fishes (Mark 14:22).

read for recurring or absent themes to help identify writers' concerns and the questions they find interesting. Reading theological texts with an investigative posture, underlining key characters, events, time markers, symbols, terms, and themes equips students to intuit connections between elements and begin to picture and respond to the world the author has in mind.

Good writing and artful scholarship comprise such multifaceted elements that flexibility and creativity are integral to interpretation. The art of interpretation rests primarily with a reader or community of readers who discern meanings based on texts' intersecting elements and consensus about which interpretations are most persuasive or compelling. The intersecting elements of written documents are limited to some extent by what authors have written on the page, yet not all meaning-bearing intersections are part of an author's intentions. Some aspects of a text may be happenstance, vestiges of a writer's context or subconscious, or aspects unintended by an author yet noticed by contemporary readers based on their own pressing questions.

While the best interpretations often attempt to do justice to as many intersecting elements within a passage as possible, no one interpretation ever captures all that something may mean. An interpretation can be "true to the text" and yet not be the only possible interpretation. A text's intersecting elements are multiple, and meanings must be plural. It is also vitally important when thinking about interpretive meaning as intersecting elements within a text to recognize that these elements are not always oriented toward coherence. While coherence may be what an author intends and what an interpreter aims to find, the drive to discover coherence is often counterintuitive.

Consider the metaphor of a spider's web for both a text and its interpretation. Some elements of an article or passage of scripture may support the web as a whole or reinforce one particular dimension, yet other characters, themes, symbols, or events may create resistance to the meaning of the whole or some part. Some textual aspects, like a spider's web, may be broken, damaged, or torn out. For example, in biblical courses students become familiar with how scriptures have been redacted, edited, or copied in ways that sometimes break or shift meanings. Seminarians also begin to see that whenever an interpreter (professor, peer, pastor) offers a compelling reading, their interpretive "picture" foregrounds important elements but necessarily obscures others. At the same time, not all tension or dissonance has a negative impact on interpretation. Without dissonance, something would be lost in Paul's description of Jesus as both a "stone of stumbling" and the "cornerstone" of God's household (Rom. 9:32; Eph. 2:19-20). In fact, one skill seminarians develop is the capacity to find meaning where there is dissonance and meaning that is not threatened by incoherence or multiplicity.

Recognizing in seminary education that meaning is multidimensional and interpretations manifold may come to some students as relief (scripture passages do not have to mean what they always have) and to others as discomfort (scripture passages may seem more authoritative if interpreted in only one possible way). As a seminary student, you will need to navigate this spectrum of responses with grace alongside your peers and faculty. It can be reassuring that the authority of scripture necessitating only one interpretation is a relatively recent and not necessarily helpful idea. Not only does experience suggest otherwise (as many faithful Christians have read scriptures differently), but for most of Christian history the Bible was understood to have multiple layers of meaning: at the very least a historical (or plain sense) meaning, a Christ-centered meaning, a moral meaning, and a hope-filled future-oriented meaning.[4]

Multidimensional meaning is what enables the scriptures to serve as a critical, compelling, and authoritative witness across historical and cultural contexts. The philosopher David Tracy believes the scriptures are authoritative over time precisely because they do and can sustain plural and flexible meanings.[5] Tracy insists that multiplicity of meaning in the scriptures should be considered a *gift* rather than a threat. One only has to remember the apostle Paul's unconventional reading of righteousness as uncoupled from race or gender (Galatians 3) or how Africans enslaved in the United States reinterpreted the Exodus story to counter biblical support for slavery and unmask oppressive systems of human community.[6] Learning to embrace multidimensional meaning in scriptures invites new interpretations to reach into our lives and vocational contexts as we mature in faith.

Meaning Is Dialogue, not Monologue

One of the reasons the multidimensional nature of interpretation should be considered a gift is because it suggests that interpretation is dialogue rather than monologue. Because many of the writings seminarians read are preserved historical artifacts, seminary students may be tempted to imagine that interpretation consists of decoding monologues: an author has a message or truth claim evidenced in

4. See David C. Steinmetz, "The Superiority of Pre-critical Exegesis," 26–38 in *The Theological Interpretation of Scripture: Classic and Contemporary Readings*, ed. Stephen E. Fowl (Malden, MA: Blackwell, 1997).

5. David Tracy, *Plurality and Ambiguity: Hermeneutics, Religion, Hope* (San Francisco: Harper & Row, 1987), 13–15.

6. See Renita J. Weems, "Re-reading for Liberation: African American Women and the Bible," 27–39 in *Voices From the Margin: Interpreting the Bible in the Third World*, ed. R. S. Sugirtharajah (Maryknoll, NY: Orbis Books, 2006) and Vincent L. Wimbush, "The Bible and African Americans: an Outline of an Interpretive History," 26–38 in *The Theological Interpretation of Scripture: Classic and Contemporary Readings*, ed. Stephen E. Fowl (Malden, MA: Blackwell, 1997).

what they write down. When theological texts are read as monologues, however, they can feel like abrasive and even abusive intrusions of a seemingly all-knowing divine voice from nowhere. Instead, all forms of communication are significant in human experience not because they preserve any individual's cognitive ideas but because what writers say communicates their own complex interactions with their world and their desire to share this with others. Meaning is multidimensional because writing is evidence of a dialogue between an author and the author's circumstances and audiences, and thereafter a dialogue between what is written down and all subsequent readers.

When I read and teach theology, I keep in mind Paul Tillich's description of theology as a discipline focused on questions of ultimate concern.[7] Theologians are interested in questions alive for them in their present situations and in human experience at its widest possible frames of reference. Theological writers have always been interested in the most pressing human questions. Is there a God? Why are we here? Why is there suffering and violence in the world? Is creation broken, and can it be mended? Whenever a writer addresses these types of questions and seeks responses that draw upon religious understandings or perspectives, that writer is speaking theologically. Oftentimes one of the most helpful questions to ask in reading theological sources meaningfully is: "What questions of ultimate concern animate this author?"

Theological writers also approach questions of ultimate concern from within their own experiences and specific pastoral realities. For example, Paul Tillich's questions of ultimate concern included "how is faith related to human courage?" To miss the connection between this question and Tillich's pastoral experience of the anxieties and

---

7. Paul Tillich, *Systematic Theology*, vol. 1 (Chicago: University of Chicago Press, 1967), 11–15.

despair of twentieth-century Western people is to miss the genius of his definition of faith as "the courage to accept acceptance."[8] Reading theological writers with sympathy begins by taking the relationship between their own questions and contexts as seriously as we take our own and seeing the connections between their questions and ours. This does not mean that you as a reader can put yourself into the mind of an author, or that anyone can project himself or herself into a particular author's cultural world, but it does mean that reading meaningfully is a call to listen and learn from the theological insights that arose for authors pastorally engaged in the most pressing theological questions of their time. Learning to read meaningfully involves respecting both the fruit of this interpretive labor and its process.

The dialogue between an author's questions and contexts is also oriented toward other readers or audiences, whether real or imagined. In historical texts and theological writing, intended audiences have shaped what writers have said and why they felt it was important. Authors are not writing monologues in sound-proof time capsules but responding to what people around them have already suggested and written; what "I say" and write is in dialogue with what "they say."[9] Reading meaningfully involves noticing when an author is describing someone else's position and when the author is speaking in her own voice. Though academic writers and faculty are not always explicit about the audiences or standpoints they are addressing, interpreters must skillfully intuit who an author may have in mind. Meaning-making goes awry when readers lose sight of nuanced clues about who is speaking, the intended audience(s), and the big-picture argument the author hopes to make.

8. Paul Tillich, *The Courage to Be* (New Haven: Yale University Press, 1952), 172–90.
9. Gerald Graff and Cathy Birkenstein, *They Say / I Say: The Moves that Matter in Academic Writing* (New York: W. W. Norton & Co., 2010).

While written documents bear evidence of an author's dialogue with particular circumstances and audiences, interpretation is also the dialogue that unfolds between what you read and your own experience. The literary and biblical philosopher Paul Ricoeur stressed that interpretation begins with "guesses" and questions stemming from what a reader already knows. Questions are posed from within our pre-understanding and tested by seasoned examination and explanation of what the structure and content of a text suggest. The process of explanation then moves a reader toward more comprehensive understanding, which in turn raises new questions.[10] Like other philosophers, Ricoeur imagined interpreters' progression through interconnected steps toward enhanced and nuanced understanding as a "hermeneutic circle." In the interactions of interpretation, reading impacts our understanding and shapes our ongoing learning. Meaning-making is the process of coming to understanding as you interpret.

In step with Ricoeur, David Tracy pictures interpretation as conversation, because conversation and interpretation are both propelled by questions. When interpretation is conversation with a text, we have to "lose ourselves in the questioning provoked by the text."[11] In a way similar to what happens in conversation, both parties surrender the desire to control the outcomes. Meaningful interpretation, therefore, is not about excavating what an author said or meant to say, but rather articulating the claims writing makes on our lives and our informed responses to those claims.

Interpretation never bypasses our own questions and predispositions but rather depends upon them. Tracy writes that interpretation only stops when there are no more relevant questions

---

10. Paul Ricoeur, *Interpretation Theory: Discourse and the Surplus of Meaning* (Fort Worth: Texas Christian University Press, 1976), 71–88 and Tracy, *Plurality and Ambiguity*, 39.
11. Tracy, *Plurality and Ambiguity*, 19.

to ask, when we have found truth to be "the reality we know through our best interpretations."[12] For some seminarians, this invitation to involve ourselves in meaning-making interpretation may feel too subjective or relative. Theologian Letty Russell insists that inviting ourselves into interpretation does not mean that "everything is *relative*" but "that everything is *related*."[13] Theological meaning involves how we live our lives and the perspectives that shape who we are and know ourselves to be. My own conviction is that God's presence and word come to human beings through the Spirit's guidance of our coming into understanding through interpretation. How would this guidance work its way in our hearts and lives if it were monologue rather than dialogue?

Meaning is a Spirit-filled Mindset, not a Static Method

The question-driven conversational dynamic of meaning-making in seminary education is often guided by specific interpretive tools or methods. In some cases, these methods are pictured for students by grouping those that seek meaning "behind the text" for historical approaches to interpretation, meaning "within the text" for literary approaches to interpretation, and meaning "in front of the text" for reader- and community-oriented hermeneutical approaches.[14] Each method privileges certain types of questions and desired outcomes that are not always made explicit.[15] Historical methods seek

---

12. Ibid., 25, 48.
13. Letty M. Russell, *Household of Freedom: Authority in Feminist Theology*, The 1986 Annie Kinkead Warfield Lectures (Philadelphia: Westminster Press, 1987), 31.
14. See Bernard C. Lategan, "Hermeneutics," 149–54 in *The Anchor Bible Dictionary*, ed. David Noel Freedman (New York: Doubleday, 1992) and W. Randolph Tate, *Biblical Interpretation: An Integrated Approach*, 3rd ed. (Grand Rapids: Baker, 2011).
15. For an introduction to biblical methods and their aims, see Stephen R. Haynes and Steven L. McKenzie, *To Each its Own Meaning: An Introduction to Biblical Criticisms and Their Application* (Louisville: Westminster John Knox, 1993).

interpretations that explain what most probably happened in the past, accounting for as much historical evidence as possible. Literary methods seek interpretations that are in tune with how stories are formed and shaped on the page; they are more interested in linguistic artfulness than historical probabilities. Reader- and community-oriented approaches to interpretation seek interpretations that shift the perspectives and actions of readers; they are interested in readings that prove useful with respect to certain communities and commitments.

When students come across interpretations in books or lectures that generate discomfort, it is helpful to identity the approach to meaning probably guiding the author or instructor. As you align yourself with particular approaches, you will feel moments of resonance and dissonance with other interpreters or methods. Reflective recognition of both resonance and dissonance illuminates blind spots, generates insights, and clarifies convictions—all essential to theological depth and responsible ministry.

While grouping methods around meaning behind, within, and in front of texts can helpfully categorize *types* of interpretive methods and their respective *aims*, these groupings can be misleading. (1) This grouping of methods sometimes falsely suggests that meaning is a static attribute of texts that various methods are designed to extract. We know, however, that meaning-making is not extraction but dialogue; meaning is not something texts contain but rather an interactive mindset we bring to our reading and interpretations. (2) This picture of interpretive approaches can suggest meaning-making should sequentially move from historical matters to literary concerns to application for contemporary readers, with each as the precursor and foundation for the next. This can be a naïve assumption.[16] (3)

---

16. For example, historical questions are only important if communities decide to privilege them, literary dynamics of texts reveal vestiges of their historical contexts, and contemporary reader-

Even though the various methods grouped in this way can assist interpreters, they sometimes obscure theological meaning rather than clarify it. The reason for this is that most interpretive methods and tools come from disciplines that are not specifically concerned with theological meaning.

The very questions that should interest seminarians are sometimes nowhere to be found in these methodological tools. The questions the methods often obscure include: Where is God's voice in this passage? What truth or insight is revealed for Christian communities today? What does this interpretation mean for how I model my life in the pattern of Jesus? Where is the Spirit present in my process of interpretation? How would the Spirit guide me through this text in pastoring Christian communities?

Rather than discard the methods that appear throughout seminary education because they sometimes neglect the most important theological questions, I use two skills intentionally. One is to connect the concerns of all three types of methods to my own theological commitments. Historical methods are important because they honor God's revelatory presence in the past; God cares about human history and is engaged in the history of the world God created and intends to save. Literary methods are important because they honor God's revelatory presence in the human realities disclosed by texts. Writing is a living expression of human creativity that depicts the world as it is or as it should be; I follow a God intimately engaged in human experience and known to speak through human voices. Reader- and community-oriented methods are important because they honor God's revelatory presence in the hoped-for future of the world; I believe God is invested in moving people and communities toward

centered questions have already been shaped by historical patterns that preceded them. As a circular rather than linear process of understanding, meaning-making is at its best when interpreters recognize the important and intersecting concerns of all three.

conversion and change so that God's intentions for the world become visible. Finding ways to connect various interpretive methods to your own theological convictions as they mature is essential to discovering the usefulness and power of historical, literary, and reader approaches to meaning.

A second skill is equally important. Rather than imagining hermeneutics on a linear plane where meaning is sought only behind, within, or in front of a text, I picture the methods particular to historical, textual, and reader-oriented approaches as each forming one part of an interlocking triad. Theological understanding resides not in privileging one realm of meaning—historical, literary, reader—over another but in discovering through the Spirit's guidance the scriptural meanings residing in the tensions that evolve when attention to the past, present, and future are in play.

It is my conviction that the intersections between what a text meant, what it means, and what it makes possible are the basis of a dynamic process of interpretation that relies on the Spirit. This dynamic process holds in tension what a scripture passage affirms about the world as God's creation unfolding historically, what it reveals about the complexity of human existence, and what it projects as hope for the future. The intersections "in-between" always create new patterns of interpretation because of the constantly shifting experience of communities and their contexts. Apart from the Spirit's prompting, the Spirit's guidance, and often the Spirit's emboldening, theological interpretation risks falling into old wineskins that are rarely serviceable or inspirational. Only the Spirit can gift us with the spiritual openness to discover the generative space that leads to the right word for the right situation, and the word that uncovers our need for grace as we seek to love one another. Seminary education helps us recognize the Spirit's leading in the discernment of meaning-making even as we tackle proficiency in many types of interpretive methods.

Meaning-making and the Postures of Ministry

I began this chapter on reading meaningfully by affirming two important truths: you already know how to read, and in seminary you will find and refine new skills you need to read meaningfully and interpret theologically. Reading theologically involves discerning and deciphering the truthful insights of writers who have theological meaning in mind. It also means bringing theological lenses to academic and literary writers whose primary interests are not theological. Theological education opens a door into the academic and spiritual formation you need to discern theological insight across a lifetime of learning and breadth of reading. Theological education opens this door by connecting the postures of good theological interpretation to the postures of responsive and wise Christian leadership. Interpretation is an exploration and process of inquiry intimately connected to good habits and virtues of ministry.

First, meaningful interpretation is the practice of *listening with openness*. Paying attention to what people say and what they hope to communicate is vital to good reading and good pastoral presence. Listening empathetically with a genuine posture of open dialogue is practicing Christian hospitality toward anyone with whom you may disagree or anyone whose experience and commitments are shaped in vastly different ways than your own. Listening with openness means learning not only from new approaches to interpretation but also from the wise practices of patristic, medieval, and Reformation interpreters.[17] Openness to listening for how other seasoned

17. See Stephen E. Fowl, *Theological Interpretation of Scripture* (Eugene, OR: Cascade Books, 2009), 54–63.

interpreters across time dealt with challenging questions and contexts models how we might exercise the same pastoral responsiveness in differing circumstances. As we deepen our skills in listening with openness, we become less threatened by difference and dissent, whether expressed by authors, peers, or parishioners. Ministry cannot be hospitable love for other people, including friends and enemies, unless we are practicing the Christian virtue of listening with openness as we read.

Second, meaningful interpretation is *seeking truth that has clarity and flexibility*. In this chapter, I have drawn attention to multiple and plural dimensions of meaning, but only in service of the quest for truthful insight into ourselves, God, and our relationships together. Meaningful theological interpretation is always in search of truth, not truth that is dogmatic or authoritarian but truth that offers clarity of sight so that we may remove the log in our own eye even as we help remove the speck in our brother's or sister's eye (Luke 6:42). As theologian Stephen Fowl writes, theological interpretation is a Christian practice of "truth-telling" with courage to name our sins and openness to repentance and reconciliation.[18]

In light of our clouded vision, clear truth must also be flexible truth. Flexibility echoes the insight of the medieval theologian Thomas Aquinas, who believed every truthful thing we say about God is nevertheless wrapped in human imperfection.[19] Good and meaningful interpretations have to be flexible not only to accommodate our human finitude but also to help us speak redemptive words in constantly shifting ministry roles and pastoral situations. Many aspects of vocational ministry, from preaching to pastoral care, involve the same clarity and flexibility we learn in developing good meaning-making skills as we read. We know we

18. Ibid., 66–68.
19. Thomas Aquinas, *Summa Theologiae,* I.13.1–3.

have arrived at clear and flexible truth when our interpretations "enrich our experience, allow for understanding, aid deliberation and judgment, and increase the possibilities of meaningful action."[20]

Finally, meaningful interpretation is *maturing into patient hope and humble endurance.* Every thoughtful consideration of scripture, every crafted sermon or lesson, every word of pastoral affirmation or challenge, and every courageous welcome across lines of differences is meaning-making. Take care as you enter ministry as a meaning-making vocation, because meaning breaks down when the stresses of ministry or seminary education fracture one's sense of identity and calling.[21] The pastoral skills needed to discern between competing ministry roles, balance needs, negotiate obligations, rest in Sabbath spirit, and keep our eyes on faithful stewardship of people and congregations are skills that nourish good interpretations.[22] Patience with ourselves and others as we learn these skills is intimately connected to our ability to read meaningfully. The frustrations that inevitably arise in reading for seminary education—frustrations of incomprehension, doubt, discouragement, and fatigue—school us in the humility we need to trust in God's sustenance for our lives and to form us to pastor not only with wisdom and discernment but with endurance for the long-suffering and life-giving joys of Christian ministry.

20. Tracy, *Plurality and Ambiguity*, 9.
21. I owe this insight to pastoral theologian Melinda McGarrah Sharp, assistant professor of Pastoral Theology and Ethics at Phillips Theological Seminary.
22. See Mark Miller-McLemore, "Revaluing 'Self-care' as a Practice of Ministry," *Journal of Religious Leadership* 10/1 (2011): 109–34.

3

Reading Biblically

Amy L. B. Peeler

As a champion of the Epistle to the Hebrews, I often find myself citing Hebrews 4:12, "Indeed, the Word of God is living and active,"[1] to affirm that God speaks *today* through the Scriptures. My colleagues who study other "texts"—Shakespeare, poetry, the events of history, or the movements of nature—would testify that they hear God speaking to them in their disciplines, a claim I readily affirm as a proponent of the liberal arts who believes that all truth—wherever it is discovered—is God's truth. At the same time, they would also acknowledge that the Bible holds a unique place in our studies. It is—to use a theological turn of phrase—God's *special* revelation to us, different from and elevated above the *general* revelation apparent in all other mediums.

The Bible, however, is not just a different *kind* of thing we study. Instead, because it is living and active, we soon realize that we are being studied by it. Scripture never remains a mere object; it

---

1. All citations, unless otherwise noted, are taken from the New Revised Standard Version.

becomes an agent, searching out the divisions of soul and spirit, joint and marrow, to disclose the thoughts and intentions of our hearts (Heb. 4:12). Paul uses this double affirmation several times when he begins to discuss knowing God, and quickly corrects himself: "Now, however, that you have come to know God, or rather to be known by God" (Gal. 4:9) and "then I will know fully, even as I have been fully known" (1 Cor. 13:12). To read the Bible theologically is to read humbly, ready to have Scripture challenge you even as you endeavor to investigate it.

I organize the following suggestions for reading biblically around Jesus' admonition that we love God with all the aspects of our humanity (Luke 10:27). The mind navigates the academic challenges of studying the Bible in seminary, the heart joins with new communities who read Scripture, the soul purposes to discover God in the text, and the exercise of strength translates the individual effort for the good of the congregation. It takes the exercise of all these aspects of interpretation to take up and read the Bible well.

With All Your Mind: Reading Academically

Very few beginning seminary students have thought deeply about Karl Barth, or transubstantiation, or apocalyptic eschatology *before* coming to seminary. And yet these same students want to know more about the Bible and its meaning. In fact, reflection on the Bible—and joy in doing so—is often a reason why seminary became an option in the first place. "Here I will have ample time and resources to study the Bible!," the burgeoning student thinks, but sometimes the reality falls short of the expectation. This rude awakening often stems from the differences between what she has done in the past, reading the Bible as a devotional or liturgical discipline, and what she must do in the present, namely, approach the Bible as an academic discipline.

Several suggested "best practices" for reading the Bible academically follow, organized in concentric circles beginning with the smallest details of the text and proceeding to the broader concepts. Following them leads you along the road toward good exegesis, a biblical studies term that simply means to draw out the meaning of the text. By using the tools of science and art, the seminary student can discover and then communicate some of what this amazing and awesome text is saying.

Reading Historically

Before focusing on the text itself, the interpreter must situate the text in its original context, and to do so he must use the resources of history. Without question, God speaks today through the Scriptures (Heb. 1:1-2), but God has done so in a very particular way by having those Scriptures composed in specific times and places that are now distantly removed from the present time and culture. If we as interpreters want to know what the Bible is saying—and what it isn't saying, sometimes the more important point—we must know as much as we can about the setting in which it was written. We can be thankful that a vast amount of resources exists to help the student in this endeavor. In fact, more has been written about the history of the first-century world than anyone could ever digest; the positive thing is that you might unearth some aspect of history and apply it to the Bible in a way that has never been done before, providing a new and needed insight.

How should you get started? I recommend beginning with secondary sources such as Bible dictionaries, encyclopedias, and books of collected essays, to get a general sense of a topic. There is no shame even in searching for the topic online; just don't stop there. All sources—whether accessed online or in print—present the material from their own perspective; therefore the necessity to read critically begins early on in the process.

Once you have a good sense about the basics of a topic, the bibliographies at the end of the entries will lead you to more specific treatments. Quite likely, someone has written a monograph—a book-length study—on the topic you are researching, which will give a much more detailed account of the issue in the first-century world. These books will probably provide more information than you might need, but taking time to read pertinent portions of them will strengthen your work with the text. You never know when the question you are asking of the text might adapt and the reading you had already done, which didn't seem especially pertinent at the time, becomes vital.

The final step of reading historically may be the most important. All the sources I have discussed so far are *secondary* sources, resources that talk *about* the time period/topic/Scripture text. Many of the resources in your school library are contemporary sources, written in the last ten to twenty years. This is a good thing, as you want the most recent scholarship you can find on what experts have uncovered about your topic. As you read these secondary sources, however, you will see that they are getting their information from *primary* sources, sources that are written close to the time in question. If you want to know what Romans thought about inheritance, for example, the best place to go is to the Romans themselves. Locate a few of the sources the secondary materials discuss and read those portions in context. You will probably need your professor or the school librarian to help you locate these sources, but don't be afraid! Think of this portion of your work as an adventure. Give yourself some time just to explore and discover what your library has to offer. Familiarize yourself with some of the best primary conversation partners for the Bible—Josephus, Philo, the Dead Sea Scrolls, the Old Testament Pseudepigrapha, Seneca, Epictetus, just to mention a few. As you take this step, you are grounding your reading of the Bible in its context not simply as a seminary student but as a true scholar.

Reading Linguistically

Now that you are familiar with the historical setting of the passage, it is time to look at the text itself. In an ideal world, students would read the text in the original languages, Hebrew for the vast majority of the Old Testament and Greek for the New Testament. It was the beauty and challenge of the Greek language that attracted me to biblical studies in the first place, and while not every student may love the languages with such zeal, I have found that students who devote time to familiarizing themselves with Greek and Hebrew, even to the degree that they can better use biblical resources, are thankful that they have done so. Original languages do not give scholars a magical insight into the text that others do not possess, but they do open up a depth to the text that only increases when familiarity with the languages and their structures grows.

It is not always possible, however, to integrate focused studies of ancient language into a seminary program, so if you must begin theological education without knowledge of Greek and Hebrew, many good resources exist for English readers of the Bible. The goal of language study is to get a good sense of what the words mean, and the reason the biblical languages or resources about biblical languages help in this regard is that they give you a window into what the words *meant* in their original context. Not only does "righteous" have connotations in English that do not exist for the word in Greek (*dikaios*), but the word in Greek itself has many different nuanced meanings captured in English by translations like "right" and also "just." If a student were limited to English, she would not realize that the same Greek word stands behind both. To understand what Paul might mean when he uses that word, a contemporary reader needs a sense of the options for the word's meaning in the first-century world. Hence it is necessary to conduct word studies, a catalogue of the use of the particular word in question in other instances of the author's work, in other places in the Bible, and in contexts from the same historical neighborhood outside the Bible. Your seminary might own great computer programs like BibleWorks or Accordance that will help you do this, or you could access simpler tools like blueletterbible.com, available for free online.

In this process, students should aim to avoid two common errors. First, don't assume the word will mean something wildly different from your English translation. The women and men who worked on the translation knew what they were doing, so your word study in all likelihood will confirm what they have decided, although you will get a sense of the word's different shades of meaning. This could lead to the second pitfall. Once you know all the meanings of the word, you must decide which one best fits *the context of your passage*. A word doesn't mean everything in every occurrence. What a word study will do, however, is protect you from imposing contemporary meanings where they do not fit and help you discover nuances of meaning you never realized existed.

Reading Contextually

Once you have established a good sense of the meaning of the words, you think about how they fit together. I think this is best done by approaching the text through a series of questions.[2]

What comes before and after the passage?
What words are repeated or seem especially important?
Who is doing the action and who is being acted upon?
How would you outline the passage? Which are the major points/events and
*   which the supporting arguments/developments?*

Notice that not every question would apply equally well to every passage in scripture. The books of the Bible, and even the smaller portions within them, must be read in light of the genre in which they were written. The letters, as instruction for believing communities, have different methods and goals in mind than the historical books, which recount stories of a people. Knowing what type of literature you are reading will help you craft the most fitting set of questions.

In addition to genre, it is important to think about the rhetorical impact of the passage, so you also will want to ask: *What is the passage trying to accomplish?* The intents of the passage (to persuade, to encourage, to shame, for example) determine the types of words used. At times, thinking about how this passage would have sounded to the first audience helps us understand the force of the passage.

One of the blessings (and sometimes one of the challenges) of interpreting Scripture is the realization that it is a collection of individual books brought together as a unit, in the language of the church, as a canon. Hence exegesis aimed at benefiting the church will not only determine what a passage itself means but will also move toward saying what that passage means in light of the canon as a whole. Consequently, reading the Bible in seminary is usually not complete until you ask a question like this: *Are there other passages in the Bible that could help interpret this one?* At times this will be a

---

2. For much of what follows I owe credit to my professor, Beverly Roberts Gaventa, whose guide to exegesis taught me how to ask good questions of the text.

blessing because other, clearer passages will help elucidate an obscure one. (What does Jesus mean when he cries out to God: 'My God, My God, Why have you forsaken me?' Reading the context of the entire psalm he is quoting [Psalm 22] helps the reader to see this as an honest prayer rather than a charge of utter abandonment.) At other times, it will be a curse because there are passages that are not easy to read together. For example, does Paul allow women to speak in church (1 Cor. 11:5) or not (1 Tim. 2:12-15)? These passages seem to say different things, and you will have to wrestle with an interpretation that acknowledges the challenge and can present a response that respects the unity of the whole. This is also the time to look at the passages in the Old Testament cited or alluded to in the New Testament. Are the authors proof-texting, or does the context of the Old Testament passage help inform the meaning of the New Testament passage?

Finally, I recommend reading the passage from the viewpoint of different audiences. If it is a narrative, think about the story from the perspective of the different characters. Then put yourself in the shoes of the original audience. (You might need to browse the beginning of a few commentaries to get a sense of the makeup of the original group of hearers/readers.) What would strike them as most important? What questions might they ask? Then do the same for a biblical scholar. Tune your eyes and ears to the technicalities that might be of interest to the guild. Don't forget to let yourself pose some questions. What most interests or confuses you? Finally, try to imagine the way the passage would sound to different modern audiences. Here you can analyze the passage according to a wide variety of demographics: economics, gender, race, faith status, ideological commitments (ecology, Marxism, liberation theology). The sky is the limit here.

For this to be a productive exercise, two exhortations are in order. As you might have ascertained, the subsidiary goal is to get you to read the text—over and over and over again. This is the secret of the fancy term "exegesis." It is really just a method of learning how to read slowly, carefully, frequently, and hence a method for learning how to read well. That leads to the second exhortation. This process cannot be rushed. In order to think carefully about all these questions, you need to plan to read the passage multiple times over several days or even several weeks, months, or years. Only then can it soak into your thinking, allowing you to see connections in other things you are learning and in your daily life. Good exegesis isn't possible on a Saturday night before a sermon needs to be delivered on a Sunday morning. Good exegesis is a habit more than a skill.

With All Your Heart: Reading Communally

So far, the process described has been very personal, an interpreter asking questions of the text. This is not a bad thing. I firmly believe that God speaks through the Word to individuals and may reveal something in your study that needs to be shared with others. Part of the learning curve for seminary students is beginning to trust and appreciate their own interpretive voices. Feeling intimidated by the prospect of speaking about Scripture is a natural, even healthy response to such a weighty task, but it should not ultimately keep you from the act of speaking. Seminary is a perfect setting in which you can "sin boldly" and learn which of your inclinations about Scripture are most helpful to those you will serve.

Yet each good practice carries with it the temptation toward excess. Individual insight can all too quickly turn into smug isolationism and pride. Hence, for reading truly informed by the message of the Bible, seminary students must couple the academic and largely individual work of exegesis with a communal reading, a reading of the heart, if you will. For with the heart we connect with others and when we do so around scripture our ability to hear the text becomes all the more rich and exciting. Consequently, when I am doing exegesis or leading my students through an exegetical exercise, once we have had time to sit with the text, I have us "sit" at the feet of other interpreters to learn what they have heard in the same text. I recommend a three-pronged approach.

Your own community is a good place to begin. Take your text to some of your classmates and ask them what they feel is the main message of the passage. What strikes them as unusual or confusing? What aspects of the text do they want to know more about? This is your opportunity to actually hear the voices of those you imagined in the first exercise. A good way to do this is to ask them to paraphrase the text and see how your own paraphrase would be similar or different, which elements are emphasized and which diminished. Be sure to ask friends who share similar experiences with you and some who do not. Then take your passage to your local church. Pay attention to ways in which the voice of the laity overlaps with and diverges from the questions that biblical scholars raised. Also listen to interpreters of other denominational traditions as well. If you are a Protestant, seek out a Catholic and Orthodox viewpoint. If you lean toward a Reformed/Calvinist stance, be sure to consult a friend or scholar from the Wesleyan-Arminian tradition. I have also had several students take their passage to their families: parents, siblings, or grandparents. It has provided an opportunity to discuss what they are learning about the Bible, sometimes a topic families aren't naturally prone to take up. My hunch is that you will be surprised at the insights you hear from all others around you.

Now that you are a seminary student you are also part of the academic community of biblical studies, so get insight as well from the scholars who have devoted their lives to the study of scripture. Begin with a few commentaries (four or five is probably sufficient, as you will notice they begin to be repetitive after a while) then expand to specific monographs or articles about your passage or the topics it addresses.

If you think about the church universal, at this point in the exercise you have only heard from a fraction of those who follow Jesus. Now it is time to expand both geographically and chronologically. It seems clear to many of us that this century will be an era in which the center of the church will shift from the North and the West to the South and the East.[3] Vibrant movements of God's Spirit are taking place in Asia, Africa, and Latin America. It is an opportune time for Western scholars to be transformed by the insights of our brothers and sisters from across the globe.

This step of the process can be challenging. While readers from across the global have centuries of wisdom, they have not had the same publishing apparatus that has existed in the Western church, so finding their interpretations will take a bit more effort. More substantively, at times their readings will reveal assumptions about the world that you have carried to the text from your own context. Letting the detrimental ones go when prompted by the perspective of a colleague from a very different context is, at times, an uncomfortable process, for it often demands we notice things we would rather not see. A great place to begin is to get to know international students in your own program (and if there aren't any, this might be a question to raise with your administration). How do their contexts and experiences lead them to see different things in the text than you do? Second, you can consult some of the available resources that compile international scholarship (the *Africa Bible*

---

3. Philip Jenkins, *The Next Christendom: The Coming of Global Christianity* (3d ed., Oxford: Oxford University Press, 2011).

Commentary or *Global Bible Commentary* are good examples). In many instances, you may find a sense of camaraderie with their reading of the text, an affirmation of the unity of the body of Christ. But where they allow you to see something you never would have noticed, give thanks for all that you can learn from the global church.

In addition, expand your vision into the past. The hubris of the present has no place in biblical scholarship. Certainly, advances in historical studies and hermeneutics make contemporary studies very valuable, but that does not imply that the mothers and fathers of past generations have nothing to contribute. Quite the opposite: they may remind us of readings that should never have been forgotten. For a thorough exegesis, I recommend that you at least listen to the voice of the early church (the *Ancient Christian Commentary on Scripture* is a good place to begin) and the Reformation/Counter- Reformation, but historians will remind us that every generation has something to contribute. Again, you could devote a lifetime to this type of study, but even listening to a few interpreters from different eras than your own will open your eyes to new avenues of thinking about a text.

Now that you have listened to others you may notice that their insights sometimes disagree, which leads you to wonder: which interpretations are right? There actually are many good ways to interpret a text, not only because Scripture is so rich but also because it is speaking to so many different contexts. On the other hand, there are boundaries for what a text can mean. If an interpretation flies in the face of the context of the passage, a consistent theme of the canon, or the historic creeds, it very well might be outside those boundaries. Listening at the feet of other interpreters calls for respect, but not blind acceptance.

Listening to others and seeing the *different* ways they approach and interpret the text will provide a mirror for your own interpretive matrix. You will begin to realize that you see things in scripture the way you do because of who you are and the settings from which you have come. Our particular experiences can both illuminate and obscure the Bible. In my own experience, as I've read the Bible alongside others I've been convicted by how individualistic and materialistic I can be. Those who have struggled under economic pressures have helped me see in a new light the radical calls in scripture to serve God and not money. My own socio-economic privilege thus limited my ability to hear God's word. On the other hand, I've also realized that I notice things in scripture as a woman, and more recently as a mother, that I don't see other readers addressing. That is, my gender and my experience of motherhood are critical advantages I bring when I read the Scriptures. Reading communally is one powerful way that God molds us, revealing our identities and prompting us to develop certain aspects of ourselves and decrease others in order to bring us more fully into the likeness of the Son.

With all Your Soul: Reading Spiritually

Your journey of reading biblically has resulted in a mountain of data about the history, structure, and interpretations of the text. Now it is time to focus on some big questions. You might have already started to ask questions like these, but if you have not, now is your chance. What is this text telling us about God? What is God trying to say through this text? These are theological questions in the proper sense of the word, questions that prompt thoughts or study about God. To get more specific, you might ask what the text says about the different members of the Trinity, what it says about the human or divine nature of Christ, what it says about God's act of salvation for creation or the restitution of all things at the end of time, just to name a few. In recent years these types of questions have been collected under the title of "biblical theology," but they are the kinds of questions that believers have asked of the text for centuries. Some might say these kinds of questions are an imposition of doctrine on the text, but if you are reading the text as a member of the Christian community, these are the types of questions your community wants answered. You still need to listen to what the text is saying, for perhaps the articulation of doctrine needs to be reformed, but if you affirm that this text is the word of God, it has a great deal more to teach us than historical or textual facts alone.

Students often ask me if the vocational study of scripture has ever led to a time of spiritual apathy. I am grateful that this has never been the case for me. Quite the opposite: my work with Scripture—study and exegesis for writing, preaching, or teaching—has often added depth to my spiritual life. At the same time, my devotional practices have provided insights for my work. One reason for this, I think, is that I was always encouraged in my academic study of the Bible to approach it with an eye toward its theological implications. Rigor, exploration, and even questioning were seen as the complements of faith rather than its opposites.

Yet if or when those dry times come, when studying the Bible seems more like memorizing multiplication tables than standing before the burning bush, the wisdom of the saints tells us not to give up but to keep reading. The very habit of continuing to study scripture expresses hope that God will eventually meet you there. Changing your style or method of reading may be the answer, but not giving up on the habit itself. Moreover, continuing to read with others may also sustain you when you do not have the strength to read on your own. My conviction is that to read the Bible theologically is to read expecting to hear the God of the universe speaking in this text, even when that expectation seems as silly as believing in a God who can raise the dead.

With All Your Strength: Reading Practically

The beautiful thing about reading the Bible in seminary is that you are never allowed to forget the *telos* of the exegetical exercise. You are not reading simply to gain knowledge. You are not even reading solely to deepen your own spiritual life, although it is certainly to be hoped that both of these will happen. Instead, your goal in reading scripture is to serve the church. Consequently, the exegetical process reaches its fruition when you are able to apply your text to a real life situation. I'm often impressed by the varied interpretations students will arrive at when they follow the same process with the same text. The differences arise when they think about how their text will speak to a specific congregation. This is where you need strength, because at this point you take all that you have learned and you apply it to the exigencies of life. Some situations will call for grace, others for honesty, but all for discernment. Therefore the faithful exegete, not just the skillful one, will know how to "read" the congregation in focus as well as the text.

Conclusion

I have attempted to lay out a process for reading scripture that helps you hear God's voice in the text. This is a good reminder that reading scripture is different from reading anything else. It has a privileged position over all other texts you will study in seminary. Hence, while you are reading and analyzing it, your stance—your prayer—even in the midst of detailed processes like translation or word studies should be that the Bible will read and analyze you. In the study of scripture, you can use many tools to dissect the text, but never forget that it is not chiefly an object before you for your analysis; it is a living word outside you for your formation. It is not just a text but ultimately a word spoken to you from God Almighty, and when you read it this way—with your heart, soul, mind, and strength—you will be learning to read the Bible *theologically*.

4

Reading Generously

Gerald C. Liu

Reading generously is a practice of love. In Matthew 22:34-40, when Jesus is asked what the greatest commandment is, he adapts a quotation attributed to Moses in Deuteronomy 6:5. Jesus responds: "You shall love the Lord your God with all your heart, and with all your soul, and with all your mind." The adaptation of this quotation appears as Jesus ends his response with the word "mind." In the source text of Deuteronomy, Moses uses the word "might." A couple of verses later in Matthew, Jesus quotes the Hebrew scriptures again. This time Jesus points to Leviticus 19:18, where God speaks directly to Moses. Jesus states: "And a second is like it: 'You shall love your neighbor as yourself.' On these two commandments hang all the law and the prophets."[1] The two commandments also provide ideal starting points for reading generously.

---

1. For the verses from Matthew, see Matt. 22:37-40, NRSV. See also Mark 12:28-34, where the quotations appear with more direct connection to the Old Testament texts. Most biblical scholars believe that the Gospel of Mark predates Matthew. Additionally, see Luke 10:25-28, which combines themes from Matthew and Mark and their sources.

Reading theological writings generously and reading any text generously provides an opportunity to practice the love of God and the love of neighbor that Jesus describes. Reading generously applies to written languages and their modes of distribution (papers, books, and screens). Reading generously also applies to the complex textures of human interaction and ever-evolving facets of culture that do not easily fit in shelves or on top of desks but that nevertheless shape the texts we encounter (bodies, behaviors, and situations). Reading generously therefore constitutes an act of faith, for it is an interpretive approach for understanding the written and unwritten or, in more technical speech, the "discursive" and "nondiscursive."

To explore these two kinds of interpretation—discursive and nondiscursive—let us return to the words of Jesus from Matthew we referenced above. When Jesus quotes from the teachings revealed to Moses from God on Mt. Horeb (Exodus) and the wisdom that God shares directly with Moses in "the tent of meeting" (Leviticus), Jesus models discursive and nondiscursive generous reading.

Discursively, Jesus clearly knows the Torah.[2] Jesus knows what the scribes have written and passed on to the faithful. And with his unique mind's eye, Jesus reads verses he has written upon his memory. Jesus chooses to repeat the ancient Israelite teachings in order to provide an enduring response to an impossible question about what the greatest commandments are. In this way, Jesus shows love for his tradition by honoring the recommendations that tradition has preserved as enduring injunctions for life and faithfulness to God. Jesus also shows love for God by remembering words spoken by and on behalf of God. He relies upon those holy words as trustworthy for moments of unexpected interrogation and for any event or era in

2. The Torah is a term used to describe the first five books of the Jewish scriptures, which also happen to be the first five books of the Bible: Genesis, Exodus, Deuteronomy, Leviticus and Numbers. See also Ron Geaves, *Key Words in Judaism* (Washington, DC: Georgetown University Press, 2007), 88.

human life. The commands to love also punctuate an ethic not only for Jesus but for all who dare to listen to him.

Nondiscursively, Jesus reads his interrogator generously by demonstrating love for the one who questions him. They share the same Jewish faith, and Jesus knows this. When Jesus chooses to repeat foundational teachings from the Torah, he indicates their common religious bond by appealing to a body of sacred writing they both know very well. Moreover, because the one who questions is, in Greek, a *nomikos,* or one learned in the law, Jesus honors his interlocutor's professional perspective and expertise by giving him a response rooted in the laws of God.[3] Jesus therefore meets his questioner where he is. While Jesus provides an answer from his mortal mouth and infinite wisdom, he also invites the lawyer's perspective into the formulation of his answer. Jesus quickly adjusts in order to speak with a language and in a manner they both understand. Jesus demonstrates love of God and neighbor through his content and delivery just as much as he speaks about those foundational acts of faith. Jesus both evokes the commandments found in the Hebrew scriptures and embodies them in his interactions.

The interpretation of Matthew 22:34-40 provided above also functions as an exercise in generous reading. I, as the author, have invited y'all (as we say in my home state of Mississippi) to read a passage in the Bible as more than a Christian teaching. I invite you to see Jesus as a generous reader. Seeing and understanding Jesus that way requires that the reader of this chapter actually practice generous reading, by giving sustained time and attention to my assertions until

---

3. *Nomos,* the root for *nomikos,* is often translated as "law." Hence, the *nomikos* is often described as a lawyer. *Nomos* may also be translated as "custom," "rule," "standard," "principle," or "norm." See Walter Bauer and Frederick William Danker, *A Greek-English Lexicon of the New Testament and Other Early Christian Literature,* 3d ed. (Chicago: University of Chicago Press, 2001), 677.

it becomes possible to see more in Matthew than a casual glance at the text provides.

Therefore, my writing about Matthew 22:34-40 hopes to lead you, the reader, on a path of intellectual curiosity where it becomes apparent that the teachings of Jesus happen in a particular multicultural context and within an identifiable arc of history that began long before he lived on the earth. After engaging my interpretation, one could surmise that understanding the gravity of Jesus' response regarding the greatest commandment requires a close look at the lineage of thought that precedes Jesus of Nazareth and the cultural complexities that surround him.

To put it another way, generous reading encourages a willingness to give other perspectives of knowledge an unrushed and thoughtful look. Generous reading instills confident open-mindedness to know that when we do accept the invitation to be guided by the arguments of another that does not necessarily require that we release the orientation of our prior learning or undertake an intellectual journey that results in the loss of our way. Instead, we accept the invitation to see the text and interpret it the way the author does, so that we might broaden the horizon of our learning and in some instances identify limits to the claims we have encountered and in other instances see frontiers of learning that warrant more investigation. Generous reading at its best sees a mixture of both limitation and frontier. Reading generously in fact often depends on extending unflappable hospitality to texts and authors, especially in those instances when we find ourselves disagreeing with them the most. Allow me to explain by shifting our attention to another example.

"Yes, Jesus Hates You" is the third chapter in Jeff Chu's book, *Does Jesus Really Love Me?: A Gay Christian's Pilgrimage in Search of God in America*. The chapter title appropriately describes the principal ministry of Westboro Baptist Church in Topeka, Kansas, which provides the chapter's setting. It also humorously captures the unlikely generosity that Chu, an openly gay Asian American male, demonstrates by interviewing the congregation and its leaders to gain a deeper understanding of violently oppositional Christian stances regarding homosexuality. Chu's generosity transfers easily into our discussion of generous reading and provides a model worth emulating.

In Chu's chapter, the reader learns that Westboro Baptist Church notoriously protests congregations, organizations, and gatherings that support the LGBTQI community with vicious signage that exclaims vitriol like "GOD HATES FAGS" and "FAGS GO TO HELL."[4] Chu sums it up best: "No congregation in the world spends as much time preaching against homosexuality as this small Topeka band of believers."[5]

Nevertheless, Chu musters up the courage to visit them, in order to see first hand what all the fuss is about and to ascertain how a community of faith could arrive at such a caustic interpretation of the gospel. Strikingly, Chu discloses that while his friends and loved ones worry for his safety, what he fears most is that they might be right: "What if I found that they were not in fact crazy? Worse, what if I decided that they were right?"[6] From the start of his visit to Westboro Baptist Church, as adversarial as the congregation is to an individual like Chu, Chu nevertheless commits to an ethic of generous reading by seriously imagining how Westboro could justify its hateful witness.

Chu never actually believes the proclamations of Westboro. But he does read the discursive and nondiscursive actions of the Westboro

---

4. LGBTQI is a common abbreviation for lesbian, gay, bisexual, transgender, queer or questioning, and intersexed community.

5. Jeff Chu, *Does Jesus Really Love Me?: A Gay Christian's Pilgrimage in Search of God in America* (New York: Harper Collins, 2012), 56.

6. Ibid., 58.

members and clergy generously in order to expose the weakness of their appalling proclamations and display the magnitude of God's love.

With journalistic finesse, Chu finds a way to read the community known for GOD HATES FAGS signage generously. At the nondiscursive level, by skillfully mentioning during an interview that his grandfather was a Baptist preacher, Chu somehow compels Westboro pastor and founder Fred Phelps to say that "we might be able to have a little bit of a friendship."[7] Chu even requests a photo with Reverend Phelps. Discursively, Chu documents stories of how Westboro members converted to Christianity, mostly, as one might guess, from a fear of going to hell. Yet he empathizes with their fear as he considers their stories and then positions them as departure points for his own wrestling with the possibility of salvation with respect to his sexuality. And Chu departs from them in such a way that he can voice his disagreement with Westboro.

Chu closes with the following: "But if Topeka teaches me anything, it is that many words—*healing, health, wisdom, love*—mean such different things to different people. It's almost as if people are speaking entirely different languages. And it's almost as if people are preaching totally different faiths." The closing lines of Chu's chapter precisely exemplify the kind of charity and fortitude that surface as hallmarks of generous reading and the kind of sophisticated theological meaning-making that can result from charitable reading.

Chu stands his ground. Yet notice that his position becomes clearer only insofar as he challenges himself to engage earnestly with the intractable and unforgiving stance of Westboro Baptist church. He does not dismiss the congregation for its blatant proclamations of hate. In fact, he implies that they have completely diverged from the

7. Ibid., 65.

heart of the Christian gospel. And yet Chu carefully gets to know the church and its people. He refuses to entertain their beliefs like a tourist. Instead, he honors their humanity and treats their adversarial reactivity with unusual dignity. Chu first confirms and respects the perspective of Westboro Baptist Church and then (and seemingly only then) crafts a critique of that perspective. His journalistic style embodies the teachings of Jesus.

The proclamations of hate and condemnation from Westboro Baptist Church of course in no way parallel the Hebrew scriptures that Jesus lovingly cites. Chu's reportage of Westboro Baptist Church does not replicate the dialogue between Jesus and the lawyer. Rather, Chu demonstrates faith in God and continues the legacy of Moses and Jesus by embroidering his visit to Westboro Baptist Church with enough hospitality, mercy, and charity so that their argument comes into full view but does not displace Chu's God-given sense of self and charity. Neither does Chu's generosity overtake his own ability to formulate a far more nurturing and life-affirming Christian claim.

In short, Chu loves his neighbor. Put another way and perhaps more precisely, he loves his enemy.[8]

Generous reading for us also means refusing to visit the thoughts of our neighbors like a tourist. Sometimes it might involve love for a text and author with which and with whom we completely and/or passionately disagree. Generous reading compels constant recall that an actual person stands behind any text that we encounter, inviting us to stay for a while in a conceptual home assembled by their thoughts.

---

8. See Matthew 5:44-45 (NRSV): "But I say to you, Love your enemies and pray for those who persecute you, so that you may be children of your Father in heaven; for he makes his sun rise on the evil and on the good, and sends rain on the righteous and on the unrighteous." Chu, of course, represents only one model for loving enemies. One can imagine other possibilities for loving perpetrators of violence and hate. With irony, Chu admits as much when he speaks about the divergent interpretations of "healing, health, wisdom and love" on the previous page. Yet Chu exemplifies unusual compassion toward a community that shares none toward him, and arguably, deserves none from him. What is so remarkable is not so much that Chu weighs the vitriol of Westboro but that he never wavers from the radical love of the gospel.

No matter how excited or reluctant we might be to receive that invitation, generous reading in all cases involves readiness to enter into the arguments constructed by others as a hospitable, academic guest. That might mean searching for ways to show appreciation and even kindness when confronted with difficult or even contrarian sets of ideas.

It seems unlikely that theological education will present material for learning that resembles the extreme ministry of Westboro Baptist Church. Nevertheless, generous reading calls for an initial acceptance of what others have to say and the intellectual energy to put in sufficient effort (an effort that may feel like more than we can muster sometimes) so that we can understand their words, even if after our reading we return to a place of knowing that reinforces our original position.

Put another way, generous reading occurs when we give time and attention to texts in such a way that genuine interest for them never seems too far away. Developing genuine interest does not require pretending that we enjoy or agree with everything we read. On the contrary, the verve of disagreement can in many instances compel us to note meticulously every detail in the author's house of concepts so that we can figure out the safest way to escape. Chu is not looking to remain in Topeka, Kansas. Yet he finds a way to be there and the visit strengthens his identity as a person of faith. For us his visit also illustrates how it becomes possible to read a hostile situation generously without vacating deeply held convictions. Notably, he also enters Topeka open to the possibility that his preconceived ideas may change. Moving to a theological register, a key for developing genuine interest as a generous reader lies in the ability to rely upon and offer the peace of God especially in those encounters where we feel unsettled or even disturbed by the authors we read.

Chu's exchange with Westboro Baptist Church exemplifies what novelist Gish Jen calls the "interdependent self." An interdependent self thinks collectively, as opposed to an independent self. For Jen, an independent self is not to be confused with the trait of self-sufficiency. Rather, according to Jen, an independent self "stresses uniqueness" and "tends to see things in isolation." By contrast, according to Jen, the interdependent self "stresses commonality" and defines itself and the world in context.[9]

Jen undertakes her examination of the interdependent self with respect to "place, roles, loyalties, and duties," illustrated by the biography of her father and how his narrative informs her identity as a writer. For us her notion of the interdependent self provides a gravitational pull to the various aspects of generous reading that have been discussed so far. The concept of the interdependent self is rooted in looking to Jesus and Moses as exemplary readers by helping us find a connection to the precedents of generosity they set and by helping us see them as interdependent selves. The concept of the interdependent self has everything to do with developing the ability to read discursively and nondiscursively and to approach discursive and nondiscursive reading possibilities as chances to practice love toward others in concrete displays of hospitality, charity, and love for "enemies." As a result, developing an interdependent self motivates a reader toward genuine interest as a central aim. Achieving genuine interest does not require forgetting who we are or leaving behind what we believe. It does, however, involve expectation that generous reading may take us to unexpected theological insight.

Chu embodies an interdependent self of unusual integrity because he connects his self-understanding even to those with whom he has little if anything in common. Similarly, no matter how foreign

9. Gish Jen, *Tiger Writing: Art, Culture, and the Interdependent Self* (Cambridge, MA: Harvard University Press, 2013), 7.

theological texts might at first seem or continue to appear to us, striving to read as interdependent selves will enable us to practice intellectual generosity with a loving disposition. We look forward to reading generously because reading presents multiple opportunities to participate in faithful connection with others, where the option always exists to ask what God is doing and how God might be moving in the thoughts that we seek to comprehend. Reading generously then invites a return to reading as a practice of faith, love, and mercy according to the enduring teachings of Jesus. That love for God and neighbor knows no boundaries and mirrors the best and healthiest ways in which we can love ourselves. And because that love requires the mind, it, too, is an intellectual activity. And if we desire, we can always trust that God redeems every act of generous reading, including the most insular, insensitive, and imperfect of reading occasions, as well as the most kaleidoscopic and spectacular.

5

Reading Critically

Jacob D. Myers

A Lesson From the Zombies

Rarely does a horror film offer much for those seeking to hone skills of critical reading, but I would argue that the recently released *World War Z* defies the trend.[1] Drawing from the award-winning novel by Max Brooks,[2] *WWZ* follows the travails of Gerry Lane, an ex-security expert for the United Nations who finds himself and his family suddenly on the brink of annihilation as a zombie plague spreads across the globe like wildfire. As the story unfolds, we follow Lane in his search for the source of this deadly viral outbreak as he strives to stay alive.

His journey leads him to Jerusalem, where Lane meets a Mossad leader named Jurgen Warmbrunn, who providentially learned of the viral outbreak from an intercepted communiqué from an Indian

---

1. *World War Z*. Film. Directed by Marc Forster. Los Angeles: Paramount Pictures, 2013.
2. Max Brooks, *The Zombie Survival Guide: Complete Protection from the Living Dead* (New York: Three Rivers Press, 2003).

general who spoke of *rakshasa* (i.e., zombies) that were ravaging his troops. This foreknowledge led to a citywide quarantine in Jerusalem that walled out the illness. Upon hearing this, Lane is incredulous. "So you walled off your entire city when you received a random message that mentioned the word 'zombies?,'" Lane asks. Warmbrunn explains the rationale behind this decision, and herein lies our lesson for reading critically.

Warmbrunn teaches Lane—and us who would read critically—about the "tenth man." Based on past experience in which common sense led to disastrous consequences (e.g., the Holocaust, a [fictional] Iranian invasion of Israel), the Israeli leadership instituted the practice of the "tenth man." This "tenth man" is a member of the leadership who bears the task of arguing *against* the consensus view. So while the other leaders read the Indian communiqué metaphorically, Warmbrunn, as the tenth man, read the message literally. What if actual zombies were on the loose and headed for Jerusalem? Then all of a sudden a hundred-foot wall seemed like a really good idea.

Reading theologically requires a perspective akin to that of the "tenth man." It demands a critical eye that is able to build on a basic reading and work in concert with a generous reading, one that asks the hard questions of a text and inquires into those assumptions that lurk behind every text.

The Ideology of Every Text

Every text we encounter is guided by a certain perspective that shapes the contours of the author's arguments. Moreover, this perspective colors the kinds of things the author chooses to say as well as things she chooses to omit. Another way of talking about this is to recognize that *every* text bespeaks a particular ideology.

To say that every text contains an ideology is simply to say that behind every text is an author who writes with a particular angle of vision on the world. Ideology is not some mysterious, ethereal force; it merely signifies our finitude as human persons. Ideology is shorthand for the cultural, psychological, aesthetic, linguistic, political, and even theological commitments the author brings to bear on his text. Ideology, to play off of a mundane analogy, is to the author as water is to fish—that is, an environment so entirely constitutive of lived experience that it is taken for granted. The only difference is that authors have the critical capacity to question the experiences and environments that have shaped their respective ideologies; most fish seem rather oblivious to the water.

A critical reader will begin—that is, before a single word is read—by reminding herself that this text she is about to read was crafted by another person, or group of people, who see(s) the world in a particular way. Such a reader will remember that just as she has certain political, economic, cultural, and theological commitments, so too does this author she is about to engage. This is not to discount the author's words from the first. Faithful theological reading requires that we read works that challenge our own ideological presuppositions, moving us to see the world with fresh eyes. What it does mean is that we hold the author's words at a critical distance as we read, recognizing that this text, like all texts, does not hold a privileged point of view on the world; it can claim no special access to truth.

Here is where ideological criticism can serve the theological reader.

Ideological criticism is like a Swiss army knife—it is a single tool that can perform many functions. First, ideological criticism is a kind of metacriticism that can help readers interrogate the theoretical frameworks shaping an author's discourse. It leads us to ask specific questions of the author. What assumptions drive his arguments? What apparatuses are at work behind the scenes that help him formulate his arguments? What examples are privileged in support of his conclusions? What voices are left out or muted? Is the author polemical? If so, why?

Second, ideological criticism can help readers locate an author's unspoken commitments that impact her arguments. How does the author think about and with scripture? By what measure does she move toward (or from) scriptural meaning? What does her text reveal about her understanding of God and humankind? What theological interpretive schemes are deployed? What assumptions does she make about the way and work of God in the world?

A third function of ideological criticism is that it not only aids us in assessing how a text emerges from a certain set of assumptions but also helps us to discern the *telos*, or ends, of an argument. Another way of putting this is that ideological criticism allows us to think critically about the *function* of a work. What change is it hoping to effect in us? in the world? in the church? If we followed the author's argument *carte blanche*, what would be the implications for our relationship with God and other people? What are the things and who are the persons who might be left out if such a vision became a reality?

To think ideologically is to read critically. It will guide you to constantly ask crucial questions of the author as you read, and thus it is a tremendous resource for those who seek to read theologically.

The Limits of Human Finitude: Assumptions

Recognizing that we all write from a certain perspective is the simple, but easily overlooked, response to the fact that we all have assumptions that impact what we see when we gaze upon the world. The longer we live, the more widely we travel, and the more broadly and critically we read, the more nuanced our assumptions become (note my assumptions at work behind these words). Assumptions are conditioned in us by our experiences. They are much like the saliva in Pavlov's famous dogs that *precedes* even the sight or smell of food. In other words, they are present responses shaped by conditioned expectations. Part of reading critically is learning to ascertain an author's assumptions and to allow the author's words to challenge our own assumptions. It helps if we break down the many possible assumptions into several kinds so that we can more readily identify them when we encounter them.

Race/Ethnicity

The last several decades have made us increasingly aware that race matters in theological discourse. In *Being Human: Race, Culture, and Religion*, theologian Dwight Hopkins offers an incisive statement on race and its importance for reading theologically. Hopkins argues that contemporary theological discourse "must take on the discourse of race because God interacts with human beings through culture in specific collective selves and the individual self."[3] In other words, our racial identity conjoins us to others who suffer or who enjoy certain cultural privileges on account of our race, and it is in this racial milieu ("collective selves") along with our individual selves that God meets

---

3. Dwight N. Hopkins, *Being Human: Race, Culture, and Religion* (Minneapolis: Fortress Press, 2005), 129.

us. Race matters, and it is incumbent upon us who would seek to read *theologically* that we be critically aware of the impact of racial assumptions on our subject matter.

Caucasians, especially American Caucasians, have a hard time assessing their own racial assumptions. As a Caucasian myself, I bear witness to this struggle, within which I am still laboring. Scholars from racial minorities have much they can teach the racial majority (a majority at least for the next few decades—by 2040, America will no longer boast of any one majority race). Nowhere is a critical awareness of racial assumptions more evident than in the opening words of Justo González's book, *Mañana: Christian Theology from a Hispanic Perspective*. Forgive me the length of this quotation, but you will see that it is necessary to behold a healthy racial awareness in action:

> What follows is not an unbiased theological treatise. It does not even seek to be unbiased. On the contrary, the author is convinced that every theological perspective, no matter how seemingly objective, betrays a bias of which the theologian is not usually aware. Obviously, some theologies are more biased than others. But before we attempt to pass such judgments, we must be aware of the bias that is inherent in the judgment itself. . . . [W]hen it comes to detecting prejudice or even tendentiousness in a theology, we must not be too quick to pass judgment on those views that differ from the established norm. It may well be that our common views, precisely because they are common, involve a prejudice that is difficult for us to see, and that a seemingly more biased view will help us discover that prejudice. This is probably one of the most significant contributions that a minority perspective can make to the church at large.[4]

As González makes clear, critical reading demands that we acknowledge the ways in which our racial experiences shape our theological and ethical arguments.

4. Justo L. González, *Mañana: Christian Theology from a Hispanic Perspective* (Nashville: Abingdon Press, 1990), 21.

It is easy to overlook the ways in which one's racial identity is constitutive of one's perceived reality. Perhaps an illustration will prove helpful at this point. Racial awareness is satirized—excruciatingly satirized—by comedian Dave Chappelle. In one of his comedy sketches, he embodies a certain Clayton Bigsby, who is a white supremacist. Born blind, Bigsby developed a vitriolic attitude toward persons of color, completely unaware that he himself is an African American. Though offensive in many ways, Chappelle's sketch presents a candid indictment of the ways in which a lack of racial awareness can impact others. To a certain extent, some of us have been blind to race and the ways in which race influences theological arguments.[5] Reading critically demands that we develop a perspicacious view of race, asking questions like these: How might the author's racial experiences have shaped his argument? What does she miss in her analysis when she fails to treat race as a modality of theological inquiry? How might the author's racial difference from me inform my understanding of God's ways and work in the world?

Though overlapping matters of race in many ways, ethnic identity contributes to one's theological assumptions. For many, national and ethnic markers are the center of ideological activity. Though in many ways inseparable from one's racial understanding, ethnicity deserves distinct attention. This is primarily the case because ethnicity involves assumptions that race does not. Increasingly in Western contexts, marked as they are by a confluence of cultures, traditions, and allegiances, ethnicity can be as powerful in shaping one's

---

5. The blindness to Chappelle's deeper socio-cultural critique emerging from his jokes is one of the reasons why Chappelle quit performing at the height of his own popularity. In several interviews, he confessed that he wasn't sure if he was being laughed with or laughed at by his increasingly Caucasian audiences. See Leslie Ann Lewis, "Dave Chappelle Didn't Meltdown," *Ebony*, August 30, 2013, available at http://www.ebony.com/entertainment-culture/dave-chappelle-didnt-meltdown-405#axzz2p4o33Q2d: "Men who seemed to have missed the fine satire of the Chappelle show demanded he do characters who, out of the context of the show, look more like more racist tropes than mockery of America's belief in them."

assumptions as one's race. Ethnicities are stories we tell ourselves about who we are and what is important to us. Another way of saying this is that ethnicity is a construct, albeit a powerful one. We may learn much from the constructive thinking on ethnicity by a scholar like Eric Barreto. Barreto writes: "As a constructed social reality, ethnicity is a projection of our own anxieties and hopes, an inclusive impulse to identify who we are but also an exclusive effort to distinguish between 'us' and 'them.'"[6] Such dynamics are often in play in theological discourse, and it is incumbent upon the theologically astute reader that she factor an author's ethnic assumptions into her reading repertoire.

Consider the wars and atrocities of the last century. Most of these ghastly affairs arose not out of racial differences but from ethnic differences. No longer do these differentiations fall along the lines of national borders. Our globalized, cosmopolitan, wired world blurs our national differences even as ethnic differences remain. What this means for reading critically is that writers come to their texts with a vast array of ethnic assumptions, even biases, and it is at this point that we can apply critical pressure as we read.

One of the ways ethnic assumptions are most pernicious is in the work of those who do not display a critical awareness of their own ethnic assumptions (consider most of Will Ferrell's lines in *Talladega Nights*). Western scholars in particular tend to think exclusively in terms arising from their position of ethnic privilege. We see this at work implicitly when a scholar *only* engages the work of other (Western) scholars en route to her argument. What you can do to help you prepare for an author's ethnic assumptions is to begin by reading the Works Cited section of an author's book or essay. Do we

6. Eric D. Barreto, *Ethnic Negotiations: The Function of Race and Ethnicity in Acts 16*, WUNT 2d ser. 294 (Tübingen: Mohr Siebeck, 2010), 183.

find any African, Asian, or Latin American voices represented? How might other ethnic voices problematize the author's argument?

Scholars in general—and biblical and theological scholars in particular—tend to produce their own ways of reading themselves and the works of "others," constructing communities with their own kind of (ethnic) allegiances. Guilds produce communities that inflect their subject matter in particular ways. This reminds me of an episode from the first season of the HBO sitcom, *Family Tree*. The show's protagonist (played by Chris O'Dowd) is an Irish man tracing his family lineage. His journey brings him to sunny California, where his host unabashedly informs him that *she* does not have an accent, but *he* does. This is very true in biblical and theological scholarship that has reigned for many decades: scholars forget that every inflection of language sounds like an accent to others. There is no one, pure theological language free from ethnic assumptions. As you read critically, you may have to listen closely to discern such an accent, but it is there nevertheless.

Gender/Sexuality/Orientation

In 1960, Valerie Saiving published her now famous essay entitled "The Human Situation: A Feminine View." In that essay, she criticized the ways in which the contemporary theology of her day misrepresented the human situation by excluding feminine experience. She wrote: "It is my contention that there are significant differences between masculine and feminine experience and that feminine experience reveals in a more emphatic fashion certain aspects of the human situation which are present but less obvious in the experiences of men."[7] This is something every theologically

---

7. Valerie Saiving, "The Human Situation: a Feminine View," *Journal of Religion* 40 (April 1960): 100–12, at 108.

minded reader must keep in mind: our gendered, sexed identities shape our theological assumptions.

What is especially problematic in the history of biblical and theological scholarship is the way in which androcentric—that is, male-centered—assumptions have shaped theological arguments. Even the metaphoric linking of God and masculinity points to a male-dominated society out of which the biblical texts emerged. As Rosemary Radford Ruether puts it: "Male monotheism has been so taken for granted in Judeo-Christian culture that the peculiarity of imaging God solely through one gender has not been recognized."[8] Such an approach to texts is ever cognizant of the masculine assumptions behind an author's work and always careful to note when such assumptions cause harm to others. Thus it is helpful to expose ourselves to other voices that will teach us to recognize androcentric assumptions in theological scholarship. Consider the work of New Testament scholar Elisabeth Schüssler Fiorenza, for example, who seeks "to render problematic academic biblical discourses on Jesus and to interrogate them as to whether they support or do not support the rhetorics and structures of domination."[9]

Just as androcentrism has governed a great deal of theological scholarship, so too has heterosexism. Sexual orientation, especially the inclusion of the lived experiences of queer, transgendered, and intersexed persons, can no longer be ignored by the critical reader. To ignore the full spectrum of one's sexual/gendered identity is to miss out on the way and work of God in the world.

8. Rosemary Radford Ruether, *Sexism and God-Talk: Toward a Feminist Theology* (Boston: Beacon Press, 1983), 53.

9. Elisabeth Schüssler Fiorenza, *Jesus and the Politics of Interpretation* (New York and London: Continuum, 2001), 11. In theological discourse I highly recommend the work of Rebecca S. Chopp, *The Power to Speak: Feminism, Language, God* (New York: Crossroad, 1989).

So there are a number of questions you might pose to any author you read. What does this author believe about gendered difference vis-à-vis God? Are the author's arguments heteronormative? In other words, does she ignore or suppress different modes of sexual expression? Where might you find gendered/sexual assumptions in the way the author writes, not just in his arguments? What does this tell you about his theological and social commitments? Such questions can help you tease out an author's gendered/sexual assumptions.

The Limits of Human Thinking: Reasoning

We all have heard the adage, "To err is human, to forgive is divine." Reading critically requires that we not skip too swiftly or cursorily over the first part of this statement. Because we are human, we make mistakes. Some of these are innocuous slips of thought, and others are more egregious intentions to equivocate or mislead; in either case, it is the effect we need to dwell upon. Part of reading theologically is developing the capacity to recognize errors in human reasoning, errors that can sometimes deflect you from the issue of the truth of an author's pronouncements. In addition to ideological assumptions, the critical reader will attend to the ways in which authors structure their arguments logically, hermeneutically, and theologically.

Think of it this way. Errors in human reasoning—be they logical, hermeneutical, or theological—can be compared to the strike of a golf ball on the fairway. The slightest shift in the angle of the golfer's club as it strikes the ball can produce enormous differences in where the ball actually lands. Likewise, as an example, if I can convince you that God can only be signified thorough masculine imagery and pronouns, it becomes all the easier for me to advocate against the full inclusion of women in all arenas of pastoral ministry. On account of the limits of human thinking, we must hone the capacity to sniff out tiny errors in an author's argument so that we are in a position to challenge his conclusions from a critical angle.

Logical Reasoning

Reading critically requires that we understand the way in which an author sets up her argument. Another way of talking about this is in terms of understanding an author's logical reasoning. Arguments cannot be made without recourse to some form of logic. The problem is that if we are not careful, an author will sneak tiny errors into her logic, so we must keep a weather eye out for such slips.

To put it simply, reasoning is the process of justifying (i.e., giving reasons for) one's opinions. We commit to reasoning whenever we are defending a specific claim or argument as better than possible alternatives. Logical reasoning involves at least four elements: data, warrant(s), rebuttals, and conclusions.

It's easiest to reverse engineer the flow of an argument to better analyze its constitutive elements. Thus a *conclusion* is the thesis of an argument: the new information about which the author is attempting to convince us. A conclusion is supported by *data*, which are the factual claims that substantiate a thesis. Warrants and rebuttals provide the glue that connects the data to the conclusion. *Warrants* are the rational links that connect the data to a conclusion, and *rebuttals* are possible objections to the conclusion that the author will include to preemptively counter the challenges we, the readers, might pose. We can critique an argument by carefully analyzing each of these elements in turn.

By way of example, let us consider the argument: President Barack Obama is a citizen of the United States.[10]

The first way to read this argument critically is to challenge the *data* as false or inaccurate. So in our example the author might employ the fact that President Obama was born in Hawaii. When analyzing such data you might set up a counter-claim (as some have): President Obama was born in Kenya. Note that this would critique the argument at the *informational* level; it challenges the *accuracy* of the *data*.

Second, we might challenge the *warrants* the author will employ to substantiate his thesis. This comes in two forms. A *direct challenge* argues that the warrant is irrelevant or inapplicable. It maintains that the warrant fails to move logically from the data to the conclusion (e.g., "President Obama is a U.S. citizen *because* he likes basketball"). An *indirect challenge* argues that the warrant is unsubstantiated (e.g., you might ask, "On what grounds do you affirm that a person born in the U.S. is a U.S. citizen?").

Third, we can challenge an argument at the level of the rebuttal. A rebuttal can be dismissed when it fails to grapple sufficiently with serious objections to the argument. It can be supplanted by a rebuttal that does in fact challenge the connection between the author's data and conclusion. A strong rebuttal for the argument "President Obama is a U.S. Citizen" might look like this: "unless he has renounced his citizenship, served in the armed forces of a foreign power, or become a citizen of another country." One could, of course, argue (and lamentably, some have) that President Obama is secretly an Iraqi agent, which would be an example of a challenge at the level of rebuttal.

Thus the argument "President Obama is a citizen of the United States" is unassailable provided that the *data*, *warrants*, and *rebuttals*

---

10. I am indebted to Ian McFarland for presenting this material so accessibly and for his example of President Obama's birth status in his lectures for the course "Thinking Through Theological Education," Candler School of Theology (Spring 2011).

all adhere to a certain standard of logical fidelity. This illustration is designed to show you *how* you might go about critiquing an author's reasoning. Of course, when the data, warrants, and rebuttals are all sound, it must follow that the argument's conclusion is also sound. This is critical reasoning at the level of logic.

Hermeneutical Reasoning

Hermeneutical reasoning—as it relates to reading theologically—pertains to the way one interprets the Bible and how this form of interpretation shapes one's arguments about scripture. People read texts—all texts, not just the biblical text—within a particular framework. This framework is guided by all of the assumptions discussed above and many others (e.g., race, ethnicity, gender, class, sexual orientation, denomination).

It is crucial for critical reading that we understand two basic facts: first, no reading of scripture is ever neutral but is ideological at base. Second, it is impossible to interpret scripture apart from a hermeneutical framework. Therefore wherever interpretation is going on, you can be certain that some kind of framework has always already been deployed.

Scholars and religious writers are guided by myriad interpretive paradigms that structure all kinds of hermeneutical conclusions. A text read by a historical-critical scholar will yield drastically different results when read from a postcolonial hermeneutic; literary critical approaches are often at odds with Marxist interpretive schemas. Recognizing that a dogmatic interpretation differs from an existential interpretation will provide an angle of critique, especially when engaging the work of those scholars who are less than forthcoming about their own hermeneutical assumptions.

Let's look at some examples.

Consider these words: "Protestant evangelical communities that assume the primacy of Scripture as authority and norm for the development of doctrine are particularly threatened by the postcritical undermining of the foundations of the hermeneutical bridge."[11] Note the words "threatened" and "undermining," which tip the author's hand with regard to how he views postcritical modes of interpreting Scripture. This more than hints at the author's own *sola Scriptura* hermeneutical framework.

On the other end of the spectrum, consider another scholar's argument: "In sum, when we use several methodologies and respect their differences, acknowledging the critical legitimacy of their different readings, our exegetical and pedagogical practices should become multidimentional and thus accountable to those affected by our work."[12] Here we find the work of a biblical scholar whose interpretive framework aims to be as generous as possible, so that no perspective will be occluded and thereby silenced.

We all have preferences. It is easier to read generously those scholars whose presuppositions and interpretive frameworks we employ and to read critically those with whom we disagree. Reading theologically demands both approaches. We must look to the interpretive frameworks of all our interlocutors with an admixture of suspicion and grace.

Theological Reasoning

Theological reasoning takes place when an author is making certain claims about God or arguing through recourse to explicitly or

---

11. Charles J. Scalise, *Hermeneutics as Theological Prolegomena: A Canonical Approach*, Studies in American Biblical Hermeneutics 8 (Macon, GA: Mercer University Press, 1994), xi.
12. Daniel Patte, *Ethics of Biblical Interpretation: A Reevaluation* (Louisville: Westminster John Knox, 1995), 49.

implicitly theological criteria. Logical reasoning certainly applies in theological arguments, much as it does for all forms of reasoning, but theological reasoning introduces layers of far greater complexity. When authors reason toward or from a certain understanding of God, they invite critical analysis on our part to ensure that the God of whom they speak is worthy of the name.

It is important to note at the beginning that one need not hold to a certain theological perspective in order to engage in theological reasoning. An atheist engages in theological reasoning when she employs aspects of theology to argue her case (against God). Many writers will hold to a certain theology, and this may or may not come to bear on their argument per se. For instance, an evangelical Christian need not subscribe personally to feminist or liberationist theological perspectives in order to employ those forms of reasoning herself. When we talk about theological reasoning, we must do so with a critical angle of vision on the author: does she hold to the position for which she argues? What role does one's personal religious persuasion play upon one's theological arguments? The purpose of such a line of questioning is not to tout a value of objectivity over subjectivity; rather, it is an attempt to ascertain a sense of an author's reasoning toward her theological conclusions.

It is also important to keep ever in mind the simple fact that theological reasoning is hermeneutical reasoning. No theology is ever possible apart from the work of interpretation. This means that even the most established tenets of theology, those that are unquestionably orthodox, were once up for debate and arose to their position of prominence through hermeneutical reasoning and theological argumentation.

Another thing to keep in mind is that many theologies, especially Western theologies, are guided by Western principles of logic. That means they are oriented toward coherence and against contradiction.

Western theologies tend to be systematic theologies inasmuch as they strive in their discrete operations to cohere within a larger framework. For instance, liberation theology is guided by the presupposition that God is preferentially sided with the poor and oppressed. This will mean that doctrines of sin, grace, hope, humanity will more or less cohere with this governing framework. Reformed theology, on the other hand, stresses God's transcendence, humanity's sinfulness, and the limits of every human institution, including the church. Reformed theology structures an approach to theological reasoning that must be taken into account when reading critically.

Finally, it is important for the critical reader to recognize an author's guiding assumption about what constitutes theological data. For many Methodists, for instance, the Bible is employed in accordance with reason, experience, and tradition in fashioning theological arguments. If you are from a certain Baptist tradition, you might take issue with this assumption, arguing that scripture alone constitutes the data for theological reasoning.

The bottom line concerning theological reasoning is that it participates in the benefits and shortfalls of both logical and hermeneutical reasoning. Reading critically means that you interrogate the theological assumptions an author smuggles into his argument. This will put you in a position to understand better where an author is coming from as she makes her theological claims and thereby to factor these assumptions into your overall assessment of her argument. As Howard Stone and James Duke put it, "where theologians begin influences where their theological reflections will lead them. Each starting point has its merits, but also its risks."[13] A critical reading of an author's theological reasoning enables us to

13. Howard W. Stone and James O. Duke, *How to Think Theologically*, 2d ed. (Minneapolis: Fortress Press, 2006), 61.

weigh the merits and risks that every author inherits the moment she ventures theological arguments.

Conclusion: Toward a Theological Temperament

Reading critically is necessary for strong theological reading. Some are confrontational readers by nature, arguing from the first line against an author's thesis. Others of us are more peaceable. We have to nurture the capacities of critical analysis in order to adjudicate theological positions.

To return to the zombie illustration, the most important skill to nurture is the capacity within oneself to step outside the currents of an author's logic and disagree with her. Some authors make this easier for us than others. University of Chicago Divinity Professor Langdon Gilkey writes of the challenge of reading the works of Karl Barth. Gilkey writes: "There is no arguing with this man *while* you are reading him—his thought has entirely too much dominating or overwhelming power. If you wish to dispute with him, close the book, lock it in a closet and move away—preferably out of the house. Then and only then can you succeed in constructing a critique."[14] Some writers are that good. The point of critical reading is to create the necessary space—perhaps literally—between an author's arguments and your own critical assessment. Such spacing is crucial for strong theological reading.

The questions and suggestions offered in this essay are intended to assist you in cultivating a "tenth man" within you. Theological reading demands caution along with the other important capacities nurtured through the other essays in this book. For many, critical reading is a learned skill developed in theological education,

---

14. Langdon Gilkey, "An Appreciation of Karl Barth," 150–52 in *How Karl Barth Changed My Mind*, ed. Donald McKim (Grand Rapids: Eerdmans, 1986), at 152.

especially as it applies to the biblical authors. As you make your way through the turgid waters of seminary or divinity school, I would suggest that you treat critical reading as you would garlic in a fine spaghetti sauce: just the right amount can draw out the richness of the other ingredients, but too much will ruin it.

Nurturing the capacity for critical reading will not only assist you in your engagement with the work of others; it will also help you to achieve a healthy distance from your own work. In theological education you will be asked (repeatedly!) to formulate theological arguments in defense of your beliefs and opinions. As you matriculate through the curriculum, I would encourage you to interrogate your own racial, ethnic, gendered, and theological assumptions as well as the soundness of your reasoning. I cannot promise that this process of critical self-inquiry will be easy, but I can promise that your seminary and future ministry experiences will be all the richer on account of it.

6

Reading Differently

James W. McCarty III

Context matters. We can understand the words and actions of others only with knowledge of the contexts in which those words were spoken and those actions taken. For example, whether someone thinks it is appropriate to wear shoes in one's home depends on their historical and cultural context. An early-twenty-first-century American will probably hold a different view on this question from her Korean contemporary.

A parallel principle holds in theology. To do theology well, then, requires the ability to think with people in different contexts. This chapter explores why this is the case and how one might approach doing so. First, however, here are three examples from my own experience of the ways that context matters for theological thinking.

A Tale of Three Churches

I grew up attending a small church on the edge of town in the Pacific Northwest. The church was located on a street that marked the boundary between the area's urban center and the rural mountain towns that lead up to Mt. Rainier's towering snow-capped peak. Our parking lot was a field in which I would catch frogs and garter snakes in the summer, and our sanctuary a converted garage in which I preached my first sermon. Occasionally, trains would barrel down the tracks just outside our doors, and we sang at the top of our lungs so that we could hear our own voices. When there were no trains, we often studied and worshiped to the rhythm of Seattle rain pattering on the roof. It was in this space, where I was mentored by machinists and soldiers and warehouse workers, that I first learned to read and think theologically.

I spent my most formative years in ministry at a church in south central Los Angeles, in a primarily and historically African-American congregation in an increasingly Mexican neighborhood, just blocks from another neighborhood colloquially known as "Koreatown." Its location was a microcosm of the economically segregated internationalism that makes up "the City of Angels." Every Sunday I, a biracial Korean-American man, would stand in front of this congregation located a few short blocks from the epicenter of the 1992 Los Angeles riots (during which many black residents looted Korean businesses because they felt exploited by Korean shop owners) and proclaimed God's message of justice and reconciliation. And each Sunday on my way to that church, I passed liquor stores, payday loan businesses, soul food restaurants, the colorful paintings of street graffiti artists, and burned-out buildings still bearing the marks of the riots that occurred twenty years ago. In inviting me to serve as one of their ministers, the church embodied God's ministry of reconciliation in its own life even as it struggled to enact it beyond its scripture-covered walls.

Between and during my time at these two soul-shaping congregations, I spent time serving a ministry in Nairobi, Kenya. This particular ministry serves the physical and spiritual needs of homeless children and orphans living in Nairobi's slums. In addition to providing meals, clothing, and vocational training, the ministry offers opportunities for worship, prayer, and Bible study at "bases" in the slum. Slum bases are locations where homeless children and teenagers congregate to form small communities that provide protection and other social needs. These bases are located throughout the slum in places such as back alleys, abandoned fields, and garbage dumps. The primary slum the ministry works in, Eastleigh, is comprised of poor Kenyan Christians, often people from rural towns who moved to the city, and Ethiopian and Somalian refugees who have started small businesses. Every day, its streets are filled with the broken Swahili of uneducated children, the enchanting Arabic of the Muslim call to prayer, the invigorating smell of strong Ethiopian coffee, and the sour smells of concentrated poverty in a developing country.

In each of these contexts—a small-town church in the Pacific Northwest, an urban congregation in inner-city Los Angeles, and the slums of Nairobi—I have read one of Jesus' parables. Often titled "The Rich Man and Lazarus," this story is found in Luke 16:19-31. The parable is unique for several reasons: first, it is the only one of Jesus' parables to include a named character, importantly a poor, sickly beggar; second, it is only recorded in Luke's Gospel and is one of the clearest places where Luke's emphasis on Jesus' radical message and ministry on behalf of the poor and oppressed and against the rich and powerful is evident; and third, it is the only parable that includes a scene from the afterlife. The story is rich with imagery and meaning and has been interpreted in a variety of ways throughout history.

The story has two main characters: a "rich man" and Lazarus. The rich man is extremely wealthy, as is evidenced by his "purple and fine linen" and his ability to "feast sumptuously every day."[1] Lazarus is extremely poor, as shown by his longing "to satisfy his hunger with what fell from the rich man's table" and the statement that dogs licked his sores. Lazarus, we are told, lay at the gate of the rich man and, though we are never explicitly told that this is the case, we are left to assume that the rich man did nothing on behalf of Lazarus, for we know that Lazarus did not receive any of the rich man's food.

Eventually, both men die. When he died, Lazarus "was carried away by the angels to be with Abraham." The rich man, on the other hand, finds himself in anguish in Hades after his own death. The rich man, we are told, eventually calls out to Abraham to have Lazarus dip his finger in water and place it on his tongue because he is "in agony in these flames." Abraham responds, saying, "Child, remember that during your lifetime you received your good things, and Lazarus in like manner evil things; but now he is comforted here, and you are in agony." Abraham continues by explaining that the chasm between where Abraham and Lazarus are and Hades is too wide for any to cross. Upon learning his eternal fate, the rich man requests that Lazarus be sent to warn the rich man's family of their future destiny if they do not change their ways, not unlike the Ghost of Christmas Future who visited Mr. Scrooge in *A Christmas Carol*. Abraham's response to this request is: "If they do not listen to Moses and the prophets, neither will they be convinced even if someone rises from the dead." The story ends with those words, cryptically signaling the future condemnation of those who will not believe

---

1. All scripture quotations are from the New Revised Standard Version of the Bible.

Jesus' radical message for the poor and against the rich even after his resurrection.

While the message of this parable seems straightforward to many, it has actually been interpreted in numerous ways across different contexts. Indeed, I have encountered at least three different interpretations within the three contexts I described in the preceding paragraphs. I first heard this story in the small church I grew up in during a class on heaven, hell, and what they are like. The teacher took us through the various Hebrew, Aramaic, and Greek words often translated as "hell" in the Bible. He explained the differences between the words and taught us what they reveal to us about the afterlife. In using the aforementioned parable, the teacher used Jesus' description of Lazarus being with Abraham, though apparently not yet with the Father, and of the rich man in flames in Hades as literal descriptions of the locations of the soul in the time between death and the resurrection. There was no mention by the teacher of the moral lesson of the parable or its importance in light of Jesus' other teachings on wealth and poverty in Luke. Rather, I grew up learning from working-class people who were neither extremely poor nor wealthy, but were increasingly elderly, that the primary lesson to be drawn from the parable was the distinction to be made between Hades and Paradise and their relation to eternal life and death.

At the church in Los Angeles, I taught the "Rich Man and Lazarus" passage along with several other scriptures concerning justice for the poor and oppressed. Specifically, we studied the story of the rich young ruler who would not sell all he had and give the money to the poor before following Jesus (Luke 18:18-23). We studied the story of Zacchaeus, which Luke tells soon after the story of the rich young ruler. Zacchaeus is willing to give half of his possessions to the poor and to repay any he may have cheated to gain his wealth four times as much, effectively doing what the rich young ruler was unwilling to do (Luke 19:1-10). We studied Jesus' teaching regarding how one treats the "least of these," the poor, sick, and imprisoned, as the measure of faithful discipleship in Matthew 25:31-46. We examined these stories and teachings, searching for their moral lessons. Therefore, the primary question guiding our interpretation of each passage was: "What does this passage teach us about how wealthy Christians should respond to poverty and the poor?"

Though the congregation was located in a poor Los Angeles neighborhood, a significant percentage of its members were middle- to upper-class Christians who commuted into the city to attend services. In addition, many of these more financially well-to-do members were the formal and lay leaders of the congregation. At the same time that we were studying these scriptures, one of these lay leaders began a ministry serving the homeless on Skid Row. Skid Row is a section of downtown Los Angeles that thousands of homeless persons call home. One can find grocery carts and cardboard boxes all along the sidewalks there, and homeless shelters and service agencies are prevalent. Within walking distance of Skid Row is Los Angeles's financial district, which is made up of banks, jewelry stores, and other high-end businesses. The stark contrast between the gross poverty of the people who live on Skid Row and the extravagant wealth of those who work in the financial district is a poignant picture of the wealth disparity in our modern world.

The ministry began with a handful of people passing out a few brown bag lunches on one Saturday afternoon per month. Over time it grew and became a weekly hot meal service with occasional clothing giveaways. It has since become a nonprofit organization that delivers thousands of meals to the homeless every year and is moving toward beginning a transitional housing program. In short, in response to the moral lessons in "The Rich Man and Lazarus," as well as in Jesus' other teachings about the treatment of the poor, this congregation began exercising acts of charity that evolved into a social justice ministry addressing the problem of housing for the homeless. They understood the story to be primarily about the requirements of those with means to help those without means. The moral of the story, in their reading, was not that the rich man's wealth was a problem. Rather, it was the fact that the rich man did not even share his crumbs with Lazarus that led to his eternal fate.

Finally, when I read and taught Jesus' parable about Lazarus in a Nairobi slum, it was interpreted in a radically different way than it had been in the small church in Washington or the inner-city church in Los Angeles. I taught the parable while sitting in a dirt road at a "base" with about a dozen homeless young men ranging between the ages of twelve and twenty. They offered me a meal of beans and rice being cooked over an open flame in an old coffee can and listened closely as my friend translated the story from English into Swahili. After reading the story, I began a conversation by asking them what they thought the story meant. Ezekiel, the base leader, responded that the meaning of the story is that he and his fellows at the base would be in heaven, and the rich people who pass them every day on their way to work will be in hell because of how they treated the people in the slum. This interpretation was greeted with vigorous head nods by the others at the base. The members of the base, then, interpreted the story primarily as a promise to them about the eternal recompense for their extreme poverty and a judgment on those who treat them with the indifference the rich man showed to Lazarus. For Ezekiel, the story was a promise about God's preferential option for the poor.

I have read this parable with different people in three radically different contexts. The people living in those contexts have interpreted and responded to that story in three different ways. Each group of people desires to be honest interpreters of the texts and confess the Christian faith. Why, then, do they come to such radically different interpretations of this one story?

The short answer is: because context matters.

Thinking Theologically, Thinking Contextually

When we read theological texts, we ask particular questions and seek particular answers. What does this text reveal or claim about the nature of God? How does what we learn about the nature of God illuminate God's relationship with creation? How does God's nature impact God's relationship with humans? How does what we learn about God impact the relationships humans have with one another? How do the ethical implications of claims about God reveal the truth about those claims? These are the kinds of questions theological texts raise and seek to answer.

However, these questions are never asked in a vacuum. They do not come from nowhere. Rather, they arise from our experiences. They emerge from our encounters with the divine during our sometimes spectacular and often mundane lives in the world. And these spectacularly mundane lives are lived within particular contexts. We understand and interpret these experiences from within particular languages, histories, cultural practices, spaces, and moments in life. In this way, all theological thinking is contextual thinking, and God arrives and is known within each of our particular contexts in particular ways. God's arrival into the world as a poor Jewish man in Roman-occupied Israel reminds us of the radical particularity of God's encounters with the world. God did not enter the world as a generic human being. Rather, God arrived at a particular time, in a particular place, and in a particular body—and this fact has great theological importance. Our knowledge of the God of the universe, as we learn from Jesus' embodied experiences, is always local and particular. It is always contextual.

A professor once told me that to be an educated person is to be able to stand in the shoes of another. However, we are particular persons bound within particular contexts without first-hand access to the experiences of others. While the sentiment behind my professor's statement is right, the articulation is slightly misstated because it is impossible, in the end, to stand in another's shoes. Rather, we can listen to other people's narratives, questions, and answers in ways that illumine our own narratives, questions, and answers. We can learn to think *with*, rather than *above* or *against*, others even if we cannot learn to think the thoughts of others. We can stand alongside others and listen even if our feet are never quite the right size to fit in anyone's shoes but our own.

To listen to others in this way is to practice what Ellen Ott Marshall has called "theological humility."[2] It is to allow God to be God and to refuse to let our experience and understanding of God be the final theological word. To refuse to listen to others would effectively be to put God in a box of our own creation. It would be to universalize our particular experiences of God as the full knowledge of God rather than to continually search for God in the particularities in which God has chosen to be revealed. To know God's work in the world, then, we must listen to the testimonies of others.

Listening is difficult, however, when we are not in a position that is within earshot of the voices of people who are different from us. For a variety of reasons, the congregations we find ourselves in are typically homogenous. Our churches tend to be made up of a predominant racial, ethnic, and/or economic group. People are inclined to worship in congregations with people who generally look, live, and think

2. On "theological humility" see Ellen Ott Marshall, *Christians in the Public Square: Faith that Transforms Politics* (Nashville: Abingdon, 2008), 75–76.

as they do. Thus, while there is a certain degree to which one can listen to others as a theological act within one's own congregation, that listening will still be limited by the social forces that shape and segregate our daily lives.[3] Thus, it is an imperative of Christian discipleship intentionally to seek out and listen to the voices of those who are different from oneself if one is to think theologically and to do so well. One way to do this is to "read differently."

Reading Differently

How might a person in a homogenous community seek to read differently? The most obvious answer is to read the texts of people writing from a different contextual perspective. More robustly, one should seek to read texts from a variety of contextual perspectives, including racial, ethnic, gender, national, pastoral, academic, and ecumenical perspectives. To think well about scripture or theological questions, one should actively seek out writings from a variety of contexts. In doing so, one will find people providing different answers to the questions they are seeking to answer and one might discover new questions they did not even think to ask. Learning to hear the answers of others and to ask different questions from those one has always asked is important to good theological thinking and is central to a good theological education.

In addition to including the voices of those who are different from oneself, one should regularly test whether what one has always believed remains believable, or if new voices and contexts demand new answers to old questions. A reader of theology should read to consider conflicting answers to theological questions rather than

3. On the segregation of American Christianity see Michael O. Emerson and Christian Smith, *Divided By Faith: Evangelical Religion and the Problem of Race in America* (Oxford: Oxford University Press, 2000).

simply to affirm what one already believes to be true. Indeed, one should especially read the works of those with whom one disagrees. In doing so one might become more convinced of one's own previously held theological convictions, or one might undergo a process of conversion. This kind of reading is hard work, but this intellectual labor bears much fruit once one has wrestled with a few answers or questions one might once have considered off-limits. Reading theologically is necessary to nurture one's faith by challenging it. It is by working through the challenges of reading differently that one is able to come to a firm yet intellectually honest and defensible faith.

Finally, to read theology differently is to enter voluntarily into a place of tension. The field of conflict transformation is distinguished from conflict resolution and conflict management in that it sees conflict or tension as potentially constructive.[4] Rather than viewing conflict as always negative, practitioners of conflict transformation view times of conflict as opportunities for the creation of new, and healthier, relationships. Conflict is a normal part of life. Thus, rather than addressing conflicts on a case-by-case basis in a way that seeks merely to "resolve" or "manage" the negative aspects of conflict, practitioners of conflict transformation seek structural, cultural, and relational transformations that make future conflicts, which are inevitable, times of positive growth rather than times of relational violence. Further, rather than seeking "solely for the transformation *of* conflict," practitioners of conflict transformation seek "transformation *through* conflict."[5]

Similarly, to read differently is to view intellectual conflict and tension as catalysts for development and growth. Theological

---

4. For an accessible introduction to the field of conflict transformation, see John Paul Lederach, *The Little Book of Conflict Transformation* (Intercourse, PA: Good Books, 2003).

5. Ellen Ott Marshall, "Theology of Conflict Transformation," paper presented at the annual meeting of the American Academy of Religion, Baltimore, Maryland, November 23, 2013.

transformation is spurred by the tensions felt through reading differently. To read differently is to allow the voices of others to be heard alongside, if not over, one's own. It is to sit with the narratives, questions, and answers of those who might challenge our own convictions or discipleship. To read differently is to listen honestly to the particular experiences of others that might reveal the God whom all theology seeks to discover.

Conclusion

One of the defining features of the globalized world, especially in the United States, is the racial, ethnic, and economic segregation of communities. Inasmuch as churches are representative of their communities, then, they are also segregated along lines of race and class. It is a theological imperative for American Christians, therefore, to listen to the theological narratives, questions, and answers of those whose skin color or economic station is not their own. This is especially true for those whose skin color or bank accounts place them among the most privileged in the country. Jesus' parables consistently remind us, as do the interpretations of those parables often provided by those who are "the least of these," that God is often with Lazarus rather than the rich man.

In addition to the segregation of our local communities, a brief look beyond one's national borders quickly reveals that the world is still filled with Lazaruses.[6] For those of us who live, in this global economy, more like the rich man in Jesus' parable than like

---

6. On the role of economic globalization in extreme global poverty, and for Christian alternatives to an economic order that continues to create Lazaruses by the billions, see Kent A. Van Til, *Less Than Two Dollars a Day: A Christian View of World Poverty and the Free Market* (Grand Rapids: Eerdmans, 2007); and Pamela K. Brubaker, Rebecca Todd Peters, and Laura A. Stivers, eds., *Justice in a Global Economy: Strategies for Home, Community, and World* (Louisville: Westminster John Knox, 2006).

Lazarus—meaning we have crumbs falling from our tables rather than not having enough to eat—to read differently is necessarily to be continually called to conversion. The Lazaruses and Ezekiels of the world are speaking. If we would only listen to their voices, we would learn to hear and see God anew throughout the world. We would then follow the example of Christ (who said, "You have heard it said . . . but I say to you . . .") by reading differently than those around us who have created a comfortable faith and, in doing so, might finally have something to say. Or, at least, we would know that there are others who are speaking, and then listen.

7

Reading Digitally

Sarah Morice Brubaker

The first time I explored Second Life, I got stuck in the rafters of an unfamiliar building, wearing nothing but a helmet and a bustle.

Second Life, for those unfamiliar with it, is an online virtual world where those sixteen years old and older can buy real estate and clothes, socialize, attend a house of worship, find that special someone, have a wedding, converse with dragons, or scuba dive in a barrier reef (to give but a few examples). And because the virtual physics of Second Life need not correspond to the physics of this world, new combinations of activities become feasible: you could have a scuba diving wedding in an underwater cathedral with a dragon presiding, if you wanted. In Second Life, you can also fly. In fact, flying is one of the main ways of getting around. At first, though, it can be hard to get a feel for the flying controls. That difficulty accounts for why my avatar wound up stuck, mostly naked, in the rafters of a building. Evidently, it is easier to undress oneself accidentally in Second Life than it is to extricate oneself from a roof truss.

At the time of this writing in 2014, Second Life is around eleven years old. This makes it younger than the human beings for whom it was designed, yet old enough in Internet years to be considered a well-established and storied, even tweedy, institution. People who still marvel that Second Life's complexity can be created "from just a bunch of ones and zeroes" risk coming off as cute but hapless fogeys, the sort of people who might still use the phrase "information superhighway" without irony.

Why, after all, should it be surprising that Second Life is created from ones and zeroes, from binary values, circuits that are either on or off? After all, so much of our lives are encoded thus. Human beings love few things more than producing information about ourselves, and today vast amounts of that information exist digitally. In very long combinations of binary values—one and zero, on and off, yes and no—is contained information about all aspects of our lives, not just our soundtracks or our virtual amusements but the relationships that enrich us, the struggles that test us, and the dreams we have.

Compared to that, scuba weddings are nothing special.

And yet I wish to risk a little bit of apparent fogeyhood and invite us to marvel at the fact that such complexity can be encoded in "just a bunch of ones and zeroes," for therein lies a rather rich metaphor worth exploring as we consider how to read digitally. What are digital environments, really? How do they differ from non-digital environments? What kinds of communities form around digital texts, and what practices sustain them? And perhaps most importantly: how does one maintain intellectual integrity in a digital age?

These questions are far-reaching because they concern a far-reaching cultural transformation. Digital technology has created new possibilities for being together and sharing stories. But like all transformations, it comes with trade-offs: we have gained some things, but at the cost of some others. The strategies I am imagining will, I hope, help us to mitigate some of the excesses of the digital world. They will also help us to hold on to the things we might lose if we are not careful.

These strategies are offered to seminarians, this book's intended readers. But just as most people do not enroll in an abdominal exercise class with the hope of one day doing crunches and planks as their full-time job, most students do not attend seminary in order to read theological texts full-time once they graduate. The coursework in seminary is meant to build useful strengths that make subsequent work—the meaningful work the individual student wishes to do—more effective and faithful. So our inquiry into digital reading must proceed with an eye to the kind of competencies seminary is meant to strengthen: those necessary for being a thoughtful theological interpreter whose work serves the church and the public good.

With that end in mind, I shall suggest that seminarians foster "analog reading habits" that are appropriate for digital communities. Like any other public spaces in which people bump against each other, digital environments require prudence, integrity, and care. Occasionally, that means refusing to accept the terms of engagement one is offered or, in this case, using analog practices to resist certain digital assumptions. Accordingly, I will be using "analog" as a metaphor for the slow, continuous, idiosyncratic, and difficult work of reading and engaging viewpoints that challenge one's own assumptions. For all its advantages, digital technology has made it far too easy to avoid this crucial work.

Discontinuous Values

But why is "analog" an apt metaphor for the practices I hope to recommend? Am I nostalgically suggesting it because I wish to hearken back to an earlier and supposedly "better" time, one unsullied by more recent technology? Not at all. One need not study much history before one realizes that past epochs were just as sullied as our own.

The aptness of the metaphor has to do with the technology itself. Digital technology operates by means of "discontinuous values," whereas analog technology does not. "Discontinuous," in this context, just means that the data points are not connected to each other as part of one unbroken process. Consider the difference between a digital clock and an analog clock. Both represent the passage of time. The analog clock shows time passing by using the continuous motion of the clock's hands. The digital clock, by contrast, represents the passage of time using written numbers. The numbers appear on the clock's face for a set duration, and then they are gone, replaced by the next number. So whereas the analog clock's values are continuous, represented by the smooth motion of the clock hands, the digital clock's values are not. There is no sense that 4:00:00 gradually gives way to 4:00:01 as part of some unbroken process. On the digital clock's display the time is 4:00:00 right up to the point when it stops being 4:00:00 and starts being 4:00:01.

I suggest that digital reading can foster "discontinuous values" in public conversation as well by fracturing that conversation and isolating people into separated communities. This connection is not an intrinsic one: I am not saying that digital technology *necessarily* yields hunkered-down communities that ignore important feedback from outsiders. But as we inquire into what a faithful digital life might include, this contrast between slow, continuous, "analog" ways of reading and quick, discontinuous, "digital" ways of reading is helpful—or it will be, once we investigate the technological aspects a bit more closely. To that subject I now turn.

Not much seems to hang on the difference between an LP vinyl record of Gabriel Fauré's *Requiem* and an MP3 of Gabriel Fauré's *Requiem*. Both are recordings of the same piece. Both capture a moment from the past. Neither one actually brings the musicians to perform the piece for you personally. The LP has, perhaps, a certain old-timey vintage charm. The MP3 lends itself to portability and copying. The quality of the LP recording will degrade more over time than will the MP3 recording. Ultimately, though, they promise something rather similar, and one's enjoyment of the recording depends on having the appropriate device with which to access it.

But let us go back to those ones and zeroes (in the case of the MP3) and compare them with the mechanism that makes a phonograph work.

Recordings for phonographs are made when a sound—the solo violin line at the beginning of "Sanctus," say—sends a wave through an elastic medium like air. As the sound wave carries its energy through the elastic medium, particles bump into other molecules and then bounce back, causing other molecules to bump into yet more molecules and then bounce back and so forth. Eventually, this wave motion bumps the microphone a sound engineer has thoughtfully placed near the orchestra and chorus.

This works out well because the microphone has something very small inside it that is designed to be bumped into. In analog recording, the thing-that-gets-bumped-into has all its jostles and wiggles set into another medium, where they can be saved for later. In the case of our LP record, that "something else" is the groove on the vinyl disc. The record has now captured all the jostles and wiggles that a needle makes when it is connected to a microphone and there is a nearby orchestra and chorus performing Fauré's *Requiem*. So when one wishes to listen to the piece later, one may simply reverse the process: put a record needle in the groove and let it be jostled and wiggled just so, thus creating sound waves in the air that resemble the ones the orchestra and chorus made on the day of the performance. When those waves are amplified, they sound a lot like Fauré's *Requiem*.

Now what about the MP3 recording? Digital sound recording works by taking samples of a sound—at the rate of around 44,000 samples per second—and storing them not as a continuous groove or a continuous electric current, but as a pattern of digits. These digits, at their most basic level, are either one or zero, because those are the two values a computer can distinguish: switches and circuits can be either on (one) or off (zero). That is the difference between analog and digital. Analog data has to do with continuous values, like the ongoing wiggles of a record needle, the continuous groove of a record, or fluctuating but unbroken current. Digital data has to do with what are called "discontinuous values." Simply, "off" means there is no current at a particular point. "On" means there is. There is no continuum between the two.

That unit—where the value is either on or off—is called a bit. Bits, lots of them, can be put together to form instructions. As an example of an instruction that follows binary logic, consider this cultural trope: A college student plans to entertain a special someone in a shared dorm room that evening, and so asks his or her roommate to stay away if a sock is on the doorknob. That is an instruction that uses binary logic. If there is a sock, please go away. If there is no sock, then come in. One would not need to be especially shrewd to follow those instructions. One would not even need to be a human being, really, as long as one could distinguish the difference between sock and no sock.

Today's computer processors cannot ponder the deeper significance of the roommate's behavior, but they can follow millions of these simple binary instructions per second. Such digital instructions take up much less space than their analog counterparts, and as long as they are stored properly, they can be replicated faithfully.[1] And when these processors are connected to the correct equipment, provided with the right instructions, given a source of power, and connected so that they can communicate with one another, they change our world, bringing us new avenues for online friendships, financial recordkeeping, crime, and charitable giving.

And they furnish new avenues for reading. The Internet, arguably the most important innovation of the digital age, has produced over a trillion webpages, according to *Wired* founder Kevin Kelly.[2] What does this huge amount of digital text mean for Christian theological reflection and reading practices? As Christian theological interpreters, how should we exercise discernment about what we read? And how does the *format* or *medium* of a text affect our ability to reflect on its trustworthiness for theology?

Information Technology and Theological Reflection

This is an urgent set of questions, but not exactly a new one. In fact, Christian theological reflection has often been shaped by innovations in information technology, even as it struggled to exercise discernment about those same innovations. Prior to the year 400 or so, Christians flouted the conventions of their pagan and Jewish literary neighbors by opting for the pages and binding of the codex

1. Copying ease is one of the biggest advantages of digital technology. A phonograph recording of a previous phonograph recording of an even earlier phonograph recording of Fauré's *Requiem* will sound much worse for having been copied. Not so with a digital copy.
2. John D. Sutter, "How Many Pages Are on the Internet?" CNN, http://www.cnn.com/2011/ TECH/web/09/12/web.index/ accessed January 17, 2014.

instead of the uninterrupted scroll. While pagan Greek literature appears far more often on scrolls than it does in codices, at a ratio of eight to one, for Christian literature it is almost the opposite. Whatever the reasons for the Christian community's preference for the utilitarian codex—and it is a subject of some debate among contemporary scholars—that technological practice affected how Christians constructed theological arguments. In other words, the medium of communication was inextricable from the theology it produced.

Centuries later, during the reign of Charlemagne, some Christians in Europe found themselves compelled to adopt a change in technology. In certain locales, Christianity had been a predominantly oral tradition for centuries, ever since the decline of the Roman Empire. Because idiosyncratic oral traditions could lead to unintentional heresy, Charlemagne imposed reforms intended to standardize Christian doctrine and worship by means of written text. He cultivated an empire-wide class of learned, aristocratic clergy and monks responsible for the copying of sacred writings.[3] This renewed emphasis on text had implications for theology: it made information available to people who had not been able to access it before, while also rooting out some local variations.

Six hundred years later, in the mid-1400s, Johannes Gutenberg developed the metal-movable-type printing press. This, too, was a development in information technology that had implications for Christian theology. Before Gutenberg's invention, books were a scarce commodity in Europe. As a result, a simple vetting process determined who got to read. If one were wealthy or well-connected, reading was a possibility. When movable type brought the cost of books down, though, it also weakened this vetting process. More

---

3. Peter Brown, *The Rise of Western Christendom: Triumph and Diversity, AD 200–1000*, 10th anniversary revised ed. (Chichester: Wiley-Blackwell, 2013), 450–51.

people than ever before could get their hands on books. Much as the Internet would one day democratize publishing, the mass production of books democratized reading. Crucially, though, it also democratized *interpreting*. More readers of books, after all, means more interpreters of the ideas contained in them. In a society with more textual interpreters than there has ever been, new theological ideas become thinkable. Martin Luther's notion of a priesthood of all believers, for example, makes a great deal more sense in a world where amateurs are forming considered opinions about sacred writings.

And now, in our day, those same amateurs can easily publish their thoughts in a medium where millions may read them and offer feedback. No editor need exercise quality control over what is published; no fact checker need sign off on a blog post before it is allowed to be published. As Clay Shirky points out, the old publishing paradigm involved preliminary vetting by professional experts. Only with an expert's sign-off could a piece of writing be published. But now vetting has been wrested from the hands of credentialed experts and become democratized.[4] Amateurs may now pore through a big slush pile of published digital writing, reading what they like for whatever reasons they might like it. There are some very good things about this state of affairs. Marginalized and underrepresented people—those whose voices would have a more difficult time commanding the attention of the trade publishing industry—can easily publish content, attract readers, build platforms, and form coalitions.

4. Clay Shirky, *Here Comes Everybody: The Power of Organizing Without Organizations* (New York: Penguin, 2008), 81–108.

Confirmation Bias and the "Nasty Effect"

But there are also some reasons for caution, for the same technologies that facilitate connection also inflame conflict and polarization. And here I must introduce a frustrating human trait called "confirmation bias." Confirmation bias is the tendency to give more weight to evidence that confirms what we already believe to be true. It is a cognitive distortion, a trick of the mind that makes something appear true when it really isn't or makes something appear false when it's actually persuasive.

Confirmation bias is nothing new, of course, but some digital reading practices can make confirmation bias worse and more divisive. Consider what researchers have dubbed the "nasty effect." In a 2013 study, scholars from George Mason University and the University of Wisconsin, Madison revealed what happened when they showed participants a fictitious blog post on a new technology called "nanosilver." Nanosilver, the blog post reported, had both potential benefits and potential risks. The researchers then asked participants to read comments posted to the blog. Again, these were fictitious. Half the participants saw a set of comments that contained personal attacks and insults. The other half saw comments that were measured and civil. Both sets of comments featured positive and negative opinions about nanosilver.

The study found that the rude comments caused participants to change their opinions more than the civil comments did. What is more, the presence of ill-mannered comments left participants with the impression that nanosilver was much more controversial—and its risks much more serious—than was actually the case.[5] These findings

---

5. Ashley A. Anderson, Dominique Brossard, Dietram A. Scheufele, Michael A. Xenos, and Peter Ladwig, "The 'Nasty Effect:' Online Incivility and Risk Perceptions of Emerging Technologies." *Journal of Computer-Mediated Communication* (2013), doi: 10.1111/jcc4.12009. See also Dominique Brossard and Dietram A. Scheufele, "This Story Stinks," *The New York*

add to an existing body of research on attitude polarization, a curious process wherein people's beliefs about a topic become more extreme *after* they have taken some time to investigate it for themselves.

To be sure, the Internet did not create confirmation bias. It has been observed and studied since before there was an Internet. The Internet has, however, made it easier for anyone with an opinion to express it in public and to a wide audience. On a wide scale, this means that a species prone to confirmation bias has suddenly found itself in possession of technology that lets any entitled dilettante effortlessly blurt ill-informed blather to the world at large. That same technology also allows groups of fretful, suspicious malcontents to hunker down in private groups and whisper conspiracy theories to each other.

This brings us back to the central metaphor of the essay. At its very worst, online interaction can appear to approximate real debate the way a digital signal approximates an analog signal. While such communication may *appear* to be a cohesive and ongoing public conversation between connected individuals, such cohesion is illusory. In reality, all the parties to the conversation are discontinuous. If they appear connected, it is only the technology playing a trick on us. At its worst, online reading material is not even expected to be true or fair. Its job is to attract pageviews, give the user a good experience, load properly across different browsers, and generate ad revenue. If it can go viral—inspiring people to share it on social media by the millions—then it is a very successful piece of writing indeed, no matter the value of its contents.

Times, March 2, 2013, accessed January 17, 2014, http://www.nytimes.com/2013/03/03/opinion/sunday/this-story-stinks.html.

Analog Practices for Reading Digitally

Faithful digital reading is a celebration of the blessings of digital communication: its inclusiveness, its opportunities for community-forming, the way it allows marginalized voices to gain hearers. But faithful reading also requires us to challenge the vices of digital communication: the virtual yelling, the bloviating, the low standards of evidence, and the free rein given to confirmation bias. To that end, I shall conclude by offering a few suggested "analog" practices we might employ in digital environments. They evoke and long for a public space in which publishing has been democratized but claims are weighed a bit more carefully, and the public conversation has not fractured quite so much.

1. Take responsibility for which authorities we heed.

Most readers of this essay probably enjoy lives far more comfortable than that of an early medieval peasant. Yet most of us have also been assigned a chore that a medieval peasant was never assigned: choosing an authority. In our discontinuous, contested, fractured public sphere, self-styled authorities abound. Even if we would prefer not to do so, we must negotiate that abundance. A peasant living in Charlemagne's Europe, by contrast, need not have given the matter much thought, because she had little choice in the matter anyway. Having choices can be wonderful, but it can also be tiring and provoke a great deal of anxiety. It can be tempting to just pick an authority and stick with it, right or wrong, just so the matter can be settled.

I suggest, though, that faithful digital reading requires us to take more responsibility than that. I think we ought to notice which authorities we are already heeding and then ask ourselves: "What are my reasons for investing this person with authority? Are they persuasive? What would cause me to stop investing this person with authority?" (To use an absurd example: I would stop investing my pastor with authority if I discovered that she was a paid actor and that in her real *persona* she enjoyed kicking puppies for amusement.) And a final step: we must try to position ourselves so that we would hear about that revelation should it prove to be true. We cannot do this perfectly, of course, but we should at least not do the opposite: seal ourselves off from any evidence that might trouble our confidence in the authorities we currently enjoy listening to.

2. Every so often, read for some other reason than confirming what you already know.

Arguably, the best thing about the Internet is its capacity to facilitate encounters between very different people, encounters that might lead to mutual empathy. Yet such encounters usually involve discomfort, disorientation, and hard work. By contrast, it is all too easy to indulge confirmation bias by mindlessly reading only the digital content that gives me the cheap thrill of feeling I have been right all along. (The thrill can be cheap, by the way, even if the content is challenging.)

I suggest that we should make a regular practice of seeking something other than that cheap thrill. We might even keep regular appointments: once a month, I shall read something that strikes me as challenging, quixotic, or even abhorrent. I will not issue rebuttals or engage in debate, let alone engage in flame wars. I will just read, without responding, and see what happens. As uncomfortable as this can be, it takes advantage of the fact that people very different from me are only a couple of clicks away. Equally importantly, it reminds me of what the Internet all too often conceals: texts and the interpretations they contain do not exist solely to maximize my reading pleasure or simply to confirm my convictions.

3. Notice how vetting happens for us, and take as much responsibility as we can.

This one is a bit tricky, because two of the most popular websites—Facebook and Google—are presuming to do our vetting for us, presenting us with content that our web surfing history suggests we will enjoy. We may not realize any vetting is happening; we may only wonder why our search results and Facebook timelines seem so obligingly aligned with our interests and views.

One can work around this, but it must be done deliberately. On Facebook, I have created a friends list of people with whom I know I have serious theological disagreements. Every so often, I make a point of catching up on posts from the friends in that list. On Google, if I am searching for information on a controversial topic, I occasionally use the private browsing function. In private browsing, the browser does not remember my search history and cannot as easily tailor the results to suit what I like to see. Those practices allow me to exercise responsibility for how I vet content rather than ceding that responsibility to a website's algorithm.

4. Scrutinize the arguments and evidence given by those with whom we instinctively agree.

Scrutinizing an opponent's argument is easy, almost as easy as *forgetting* to scrutinize the argument of a like-minded person. While I do not keep any sort of running tally, I try to match each criticism of an ideological opponent's position with an equally rigorous criticism of a position or person I agree with. If I have demanded that an opponent support her claims with peer-reviewed studies no more than five years old, I should then ask myself: have I required the same of the people I typically agree with? Or do I just assume that the current research probably exists somewhere? Should I not try to run each argument through the same tests and hold them to the same standards? Cognitive bias tempts us to be lazy about opinions we "just know" to be right. Digital environments provide few checks on such laziness. Resist that.

I offer these four suggestions as spiritual disciplines of faithful reading. Most readers will probably be able to think of several more that suit their own digital lives and reading habits. All of these suggestions are intended to form people who are accountable, truthful, and charitable. They are meant to form people whose digital interactions proceed in good faith. They do not, however, promise to be *effective,* if by "effective" one means "helpful for winning a debate and getting one's way online." Classically, this has not been the point of spiritual disciplines like pilgrimage, fasting, meditative prayer, almsgiving, and so forth. To the extent that they "work," that work happens in many moments, over the course of a life—or even (dare I say) a Second Life?—as a certain kind of person develops a certain kind of character. This sort of character reveals itself slowly. It costs much more, in time and labor, than it would cost a Second Life developer to make you the custom dragon avatar for the wedding. But the result is a character that can navigate more than just texts, more than binary data, more than just digital approximations. The result is a character that can navigate a faithful *real* life, whether online or off.

8

Reading Spiritually

Shanell T. Smith

"Oh. My. Gosh! What have I gotten myself into? This is not what I expected. This is not like the Bible studies we have at church. Did somebody just say 'that *man*, Jesus?!' ... And all this reading?! How am I ever going to be able to retain this? How is this overload and bombarding of 'religious' material supposed to help me grow spiritually? Ugh!"

Welcome to seminary.

These thoughts recurred in my mind during my first year of seminary training. I had applied to seminary to get closer to Jesus and to get ordained so that I could preach to the masses; however, it felt as if the vast amount of *information* I was receiving was hindering my need for spiritual *formation*. It seemed as if all the information I received *about* God began to get in the way of my relationship *with* God and my desire to learn how to carry out my ministry more faithfully. What was I going to do? From where would my help come?

If you have experienced what I describe above—or have yet to (wait for it!)—do not be discouraged. I would like to suggest a strategy for you, which is helpfully encapsulated in the acronym "S.o. W.h.a.t?." This strategy will help you to read *spiritually*, that is, to slow down the speeding learning train just long enough to take in the religious landscape and ask, "What does God want me to take from this?" Reading spiritually involves not only being intentionally reflective about the texts you read (both religious and non-religious) but also being appreciative readers of your colleagues and their religious purview. This approach enhances the learning of the self and deepens your connection with God *as you read*. Notice that reading spiritually is not the same as reading devotionally. Neither is it a non-academic or non-critical exercise. Let me state from the outset that reading spiritually is both a religious *and* an academic task. These two understandings are not in a dichotomous relationship that is forever in tension. Instead, they are two fluid concepts held in tandem, that is, in partnership with each other. This is what reading spiritually is about.

The "S.o. W.h.a.t?" plan asks the obvious question, "So what?" As you read, encounter others in dialogue, and engage in hermeneutical exercises, ask yourself, "Why does this matter?" and then, "Why does or should this matter *to me* and the religious community I serve?" These two basic "so what?" questions will keep you on your spiritual path. They help you not only to keep your learning focused but also to tease out and take note of the things that resonate with your ultimate goals, your needs, and your spiritual development.

But there is a word of caution to be shared here. Asking "so what?" does not mean we are to negate, discard, or ignore information or people that seek to challenge or stretch us. Neither does it mean that we can discard readings or learning that do not appear to apply to our own immediate questions. That is, asking "why does this matter?" is not a narrowing of learning but a way to open it up. We must engage in dialogue especially when the outcome is to seek understanding or is an attempt to help us develop or mature theologically.

Reading spiritually, that is, asking "S.o. W.h.a.t?" involves an interrelated set of processes. I will present them step-by-step, but these practices are sure to overlap and are quite fluid in nature. Let's get started.

"S.o. What?" The "S" refers to **self-reflection**. When we read texts—especially sacred texts—we never do so objectively. We are flesh-and-blood readers.[1] This means that when we approach texts for spiritual enlightenment, we come bearing our "stuff"—our presuppositions, biases, stereotypes, etc.—whether or not we are aware of them. The experiences (both good and bad) and the teaching or training we have received not only color the way we read texts spiritually but also influence the questions we bring to the task of biblical interpretation. Self-reflection involves taking inventory of the self and the communities that formed us.

Several factors affect how we read spiritually. Some of these factors include, but are not limited to, one's religious tradition (especially one's denominational tradition), the role and teaching of one's pastor and other religious mentors, gender, ethnicity, political stance, and childhood rearing.[2] These factors will guide your thinking, helping you to formulate certain questions but perhaps also precluding you

1. With regard to flesh-and-blood readers, New Testament scholar Fernando F. Segovia writes: "all . . . readers are themselves regarded as variously positioned and engaged in their own respective social locations" ("Cultural Studies and Contemporary Biblical Criticism: Ideological Criticism as Mode of Discourse," 1–17 in *Reading from this Place*, vol. 2, *Social Location and Biblical Interpretation in Global Perspective*, ed. Fernando F. Segovia and Mary Ann Tolbert [Minneapolis: Fortress Press, 2000]), at 7.
2. For a more detailed list of factors to consider in your self-reflection see Norman K. Gottwald, "Framing Biblical Interpretation at New York Theological Seminary: A Student Self-Inventory on Biblical Hermeneutics," in *Reading from This Place,* vol. 1, *Social Location and Biblical Interpretation in the United States,* eds. Fernando F. Segovia and Mary Ann Tolbert (Minneapolis: Fortress Press, 1995), 251–61.

from asking others. They will prompt you to seek answers in texts that speak specifically to what you know and what you have known to be your spiritual truth. But reading spiritually will also take you beyond your experiences into new territories.

This is where you want to be. This space of uncharted territory—of uncertainty—is where our growing edges are. These are the moments when God can show us new things, fill us with new insights, stretch our faith, and enhance our spiritual development. But it all begins with self-reflection, since reading spiritually is also a reading of the self. To say it differently, *who* we are affects *how* we read. This self-reflective task starts before seminary, it is active in the present moment, and it will be a vital part of the life of ministry. It is never too late to begin such reflections, but they are also never complete.

The next step in the "S.o. What?" strategy is being **open**. Seminary can be a place where a great deal of new information is imparted, diverse people make up the learning community, and the Spirit of God moves as never before. Be open to it all. We naturally possess a protective mechanism that automatically kicks into gear when the things we have been taught or our values—especially ingrained spiritual ones—are challenged. Some of your initial reaction to what you will learn will be to reject it. ("What do you mean, Paul may not have written Hebrews?!") Such scholarly insights can sometimes compel seminarians to approach the Bible as a text but not necessarily a *sacred* text. This runs counter to what you have learned in your religious community and tempts you to establish a dichotomy between the church and the academy, but I beg you to refrain from doing so. (I will come back to this when we discuss discernment below.)

People come to seminary for different reasons. For instance, not everyone comes to learn more about the word of God in order to preach the good news. Some of my best students have attended seminary to learn about the Bible in order to refute its claims. But do not let these different motivations deter you from learning from your classmates. Reading spiritually also includes being open to the (spiritual or avowedly non-spiritual) readings of others. I have learned through my teaching at an intentionally interreligious seminary that having dialogue with someone who does not share similar religious beliefs (even among Christians at the denominational level) compels us to think about why we believe what we believe. Multiplicity of interpretation and spiritual views can function as a means of accountability and can widen our imagination. This is a good thing. This is a sign of spiritual growth.

When you are open to the biblical interpretations of others, not only does the influence of your own context come to the fore but the similarities and (most importantly) the distinctions between your views and others are highlighted. This provides us with opportunities to assess our spiritual beliefs and the ways we read spiritually. What distinguishes my reading from my colleague's? Why do I read this way, and is it beneficial to me and to those I serve? Do I truly engage the biblical text from a spiritual perspective, that is, do I surrender to the Spirit's direction, or do I get in the way? Why was I not able to perceive that from the text?

Difference is not to be feared, softened, or avoided. In fact, when we engage texts and each other *in community*, it causes us to be aware of how our interpretations may relate to and affect others. Reading spiritually is thus a relational matter.

There will also be moments when the Spirit will surprise you. If you are open to the process that is called "seminary," you will have moments when the classroom takes on a life of its own and becomes a space of spiritual transformation. ("Professor X is preaching! She truly blessed us today!") These instances when the Spirit moves will occur in the oddest of places. For me, it was in the cafeteria where we did most of our "theologizing." As I have mentioned, reading spiritually not only involves the reading of texts but also the reading of people.

On one occasion in the cafeteria, a student said rather agitatedly: "These Presbyterians are killing me in preaching class! And in chapel . . . you call that worship?" This particular student did not know that I was a Presbyterian. I informed him that I was, at which time he attempted to retract his statement by saying, "Oh, but you are different." Then I told him that his remarks were stereotypical and inaccurate. "Had you taken the time to *really* observe how 'Presbyterians' worship, you would have noticed the reverent posture of closed eyes, bowed heads, and open hands to receive what God is imparting," I said to him. Reading spiritually—as in this case—involves being open to hear the thoughts of others, not for the purpose of confrontation but for education. Sometimes, the Spirit will use the insights and even the ignorance of others to bring about intellectual and spiritual growth and change. And when we are the recipients of this spiritual corrective, we should be open to the knowledge that is imparted to us, claim ownership of our misunderstandings, assumptions, and their implications, and then behave accordingly, since our being informed increases our responsibility. A spiritual reading involves being open.

The "W" in the "S.o. **W**.h.a.t?" strategy stands for **wait**. There will be many times in your seminary experience when you may very well want to quit. One of the main reasons may be that you believe the information you are receiving contradicts what you have been taught to believe, and this causes the seemingly solid foundation of your faith to tremble. Wait. Seminary is not meant to destroy your faith but to strengthen it, to increase it. For many of us, seminary is a wilderness experience in which one's faith is tested and tried, but in which anyone—anyone, that is, who stays encouraged and sticks with it—can emerge stronger and with a faith more robust than when he or she began.

But waiting is not just passive; waiting is also an action word. Isaiah 40:31 (NRSV) tells us that "those who wait for the Lord shall renew their strength, they shall mount up with wings like eagles, they shall run and not be weary, they shall walk and not faint." What comes to my mind when thinking of those who need to "renew their strength" is an individual lying in bed, resting in order to recuperate. However, even when one is resting—waiting to get better—there comes a point when restoration can too easily topple over into deterioration. Before this occurs, we have to get up and do something. We have to get moving again. The same applies to reading spiritually.

When our faith is shaken because of something we have read or someone we have encountered, our initial reaction may be to reject this new experience. We may also be tempted simply to pause to consider what has occurred, and this is not a bad thing. However, it is important that our pause not turn into paralysis. When your spirit is disturbed or the usual manner in which you read spiritually is disrupted, it may just be the Spirit directing you to wait. The Spirit is urging you to take some time to reflect and not to renounce, to be relentless in gaining understanding, not to relinquish and abandon all hope of being enlightened, to be revitalized and ready to revel in what God has to offer you, not to be reserved in your quest for spiritual direction. In other words, we are to pray. In the midst of such a pause we are to be engaged in active contemplation, seeking God, who guides us into the next step, for direction.

"H" in the "S.o. W.h.a.t?" reading strategy refers to **hearing**. We are to listen for God's word to us. In order for us to hear what God is relaying to us as we read spiritually, we must first decrease the volume of other competing distractions. We have to "turn down" distractions and other things that vie for our attention in order to hear the "still small voice" of God (1 Kings 19:12, KJV). When we read spiritually, there will be moments when something will resonate with our spirit; something will stir inside us. Despite the unending pressure to keep reading to complete the assignment (because there is much more to be done), I encourage you to take the time to sit with whatever has moved you. Some people refer to being "convicted" in the Spirit, namely, when the spirit identifies something as "wrong" for which a believer needs to repent. But this is not always the case. Reading spiritually also involves being in tune with what God is calling us to do and taking the time to grapple with concepts and wrestle with texts or interpretations that impel us to re-examine our own thinking. It is in our best interest to hear what God is trying to telling us. Sometimes, God simply wants us to think through some of the implications of what we are learning. ("If the Bible was written by men for men, what implications [if any] does that have for women?" or "Why do some churches subscribe to a figurative understanding about slavery but a literal interpretation of the text when it involves the subordination of women in leadership?")

In short, we ought to listen for God in the classroom. God does not stop talking just because the professor has begun lecturing. You will be inundated with bucketloads of material—most of it unfortunately dubbed "academic," as if the church does not think critically—and you may not agree with all of it. Yet, I would advise you to take copious notes, reflect on them later (sometimes it will be years later), and hold on to what you need and what can benefit and grow the religious communities you serve. You just may be surprised by what your local communities really need. Sometimes "growing" the church includes challenging the church.

Some of the information we receive in seminary is immediately transferrable to the pulpit, while some of it is not. Similarly, much of what we learn and do in the church is not immediately relevant to the task at hand in the classroom. The challenge in breaking down the dichotomous wall between the church and the academy remains. While seminaries should definitely be involved in breaking this problematic divide, it is the seminarians who are most able to affect such a change on a larger scale. By relaying information not only in the classroom but also from the pulpit, the seminarian can keep both the church and the academy equally informed. Reading spiritually, then, is more than just an individual task, since its benefits are for a larger collective. Therefore, I encourage you to keep listening for God's voice as you read spiritually, for hearing what needs to be shared is an important process of discernment, even if that discernment is a lifelong process.

The next phase of the "S.o. W.h.a.t?" reading strategy is being willing to **adjust**. In the previous stages, we learned that God will sometimes cause our spirits to be disrupted in order to get our attention about a certain matter. In these "teaching" moments, God invites us to consider how this new information or situation is shaping our thinking, but it does not end there.

God expects us to put this teaching into action. We are to adjust our spiritual practices according to the *new* standards God has set for us. The emphasis on the word *new* is key. God does not want us simply to adjust, that is, to accommodate and modify ourselves into the likeness of other folk. To adjust not only means to accommodate, assimilate, or fit in. Instead, God calls us to adapt ourselves to a new way of believing and thinking about the (written or breathing) texts (books or people, respectively) we encounter. My hope is that seminarians do not leave seminary the same way they entered. They are to be transformed by the renewing (that is, the stretching) of their minds (Rom. 12:2). Reading spiritually is a vital part of this process.

The last stage of the "S.o. W.h.a.t?" strategy for reading spiritually is to **teach**, or as the preacher in me would say, "Tell it!" One of the purposes of seminary is to help train individuals to become better and *more* informed teachers of God's Word. The inclusion of the word "more" in the previous sentence is meant to highlight the fact that you do already know some things. Some of you probably entered seminary because your ability to interpret and preach the Word of God has been affirmed, and your desire to serve your religious community in a higher capacity requires you to seek such training. Others may have entered seminary because they majored in religious or biblical studies in their undergraduate education and are intrigued by these topics. Others still may come to seminary unsure of their reasons but looking for a sense of direction and call. No matter your motives, you bring a wealth of knowledge to this endeavor.

However, this does not mean that you know everything. One of the toughest jobs for professors (I have learned) and one of the most frustrating situations for students (I remember) is to be in a classroom with someone who discounts or rejects any or all instruction because they already possess all that they need *except* the degree. These are "letter seekers"; please do not be one of them. Consider your calling and remember that you are in seminary to gain as much knowledge and wisdom as you can so that you can teach *others* what you have learned. (I am sorry, but it is not *all* about you.) The training we receive in seminary is for the spiritual formation not only of ourselves but also of others, especially those communities we are called to serve. Not everyone is privileged to attend seminary. Consider yourself blessed.

Take what you learn and do not lord it over people. (Dare I refer you to Matthew 23?) Instead, walk alongside others and help teach them to discern how God is moving in their lives. Impart the knowledge you have received and allow people to grapple with it just as you did. Communicate *with* them, not only *to* them the material that caused you to pause, was difficult to hear, or enlightened you. Explain to them *how* to read spiritually (in addition to the other ways of reading presented in this book so far). For example, if you find the "S.o W.h.a.t?" strategy on how to read spiritually helpful, share it. Embody what it means to be open to the spiritual insights of others and how to be humble when on the receiving end of a spiritual corrective.

And last, when you teach others, edify them. Inspire them. Encourage them to be persistent in their quest for knowledge about God and life lived in alignment with God's hopes. Elevate their spirits when they are troubled or disheartened about information that contradicts what they believe. Lead by example. Take a risk and be vulnerable. Be willing to say, "I do not know," or if you need to sound more "preachy" say, "I have reached the edge of my ignorance." Acknowledge the fact that God still speaks and not only through professors or pastors. You will miss your blessing if you think you cannot learn from your parishioners. Teach and be taught.

Reading spiritually involves so much more than reading the lectionary text on Sunday morning. It is a process. *Before* you read *spiritually*, that is, before you read texts or engage in theological dialogue with other seminarians, take time to do some self-reflection. Ask yourself what qualities or thoughts you have learned or inherited that influence the way you read or approach religious matters. Be open to instruction—both the material presented in class and the thoughts, religious practices, and interpretations of others. **W**ait. Do not leave seminary in haste just because the foundation of your faith appears to be shaken because of the inconsistencies you noticed between the information you received in seminary and your Sunday school training. Follow the Spirit's prompting and take time to contemplate what exactly has affected you, moved you. Then you will be in a position to hear what God may want you to learn. Once you have received God's direction, adjust your thinking, your habits, or your approach accordingly. When God speaks, transformation occurs *if* we listen.

And when all is said and done, teach others what you have learned. Share what you have acquired so that the religious community you serve can be uplifted and better equipped to carry out God's ministry. After all, what good is learning how to read spiritually if you keep it to yourself?

Reading More

This book is only the beginning. When you are ready to reflect more on what it means to read theologically, we commend the following texts to you.

Adler, Mortimer J., and Charles Van Doren. *How to Read a Book: The Classic Guide to Intelligent Reading.* New York: Touchstone, 1972.

Chu, Jeff. *Does Jesus Really Love Me? A Gay Christian's Pilgrimage in Search of God in America.* New York: Harper Collins, 2012.

De La Torre, Miguel A. *Reading the Bible from the Margins.* Maryknoll, NY: Orbis Books, 2002.

Fee, Gordon, and Doug Stuart. *How to Read the Bible for All Its Worth.* 3d ed. Grand Rapids: Zondervan, 2003.

Fowl, Stephen E. *Theological Interpretation of Scripture.* Eugene, OR: Cascade Books, 2009.

Freire, Paulo. *Pedagogy of the Oppressed.* New York: Continuum, 1997.

Haynes, Stephen R. and Steven L. McKenzie. *To Each Its Own Meaning: An Introduction to Biblical Criticisms and Their Application.* Louisville: Westminster John Knox, 1993.

hooks, bell. *Teaching to Transgress: Education as the Practice of Freedom.* New York: Routledge, 1994.

Jen, Gish. *Tiger Writing: Art, Culture, and the Interdependent Self.* Cambridge, MA: Harvard University Press, 2013.

Law, Eric H. F. *The Wolf Shall Dwell with the Lamb: A Spirituality for Leadership in a Multicultural Community.* St. Louis: Chalice Press, 1993.

Mulholland, M. Robert, Jr. *Shaped by the Word: The Power of Scripture in Spiritual Formation.* Nashville: The Upper Room, 1985.

Segovia, Fernando F. "Cultural Studies and Contemporary Biblical Criticism: Ideological Criticism as Mode of Discourse," 1–17 in *Reading from this Place*, vol. 2, *Social Location and Biblical Interpretation in Global Perspective*, ed. Fernando F. Segovia and Mary Ann Tolbert. Minneapolis: Fortress Press, 2000.

Segovia, Fernando F., and Mary Ann Tolbert, eds. *Reading from This Place.* Volume 1, *Social Location and Biblical Interpretation in the United States.* Minneapolis: Fortress Press, 1995.

———, and Mary Ann Tolbert, eds. *Reading from This Place.* Volume 2, *Social Location and Biblical Interpretation in Global Perspective.* Minneapolis: Fortress Press, 2000.

Stone, Howard W. and James O. Duke. *How to Think Theologically.* 2d ed. Minneapolis: Fortress Press, 2006.

Thielicke, Helmut. *A Little Exercise for Young Theologians.* Grand Rapids: Eerdmans, 1961.

Bibliography

Anderson, Ashley A., Dominique Brossard, Dietram A. Scheufele, Michael A. Xenos, and Peter Ladwig. "The 'Nasty Effect:' Online Incivility and Risk Perceptions of Emerging Technologies." *Journal of Computer-Mediated Communication* (2013), doi: 10.1111/jcc4.12009.

Barreto, Eric D. *Ethnic Negotiations: The Function of Race and Ethnicity in Acts 16.* WUNT 2d ser. 294. Tübingen: Mohr Siebeck, 2010.

Brossard, Dominique and Dietram A. Scheufele. "This Story Stinks." *The New York Times.* March 2, 2013.

Brown, Peter. *The Rise of Western Christendom: Triumph and Diversity, AD 200–1000.* 10th anniversary revised ed. Chichester: Wiley-Blackwell, 2013.

Browning, Melissa. *Risky Marriage: HIV and Intimate Relationships in Tanzania.* Lanham, MD: Lexington Books, 2013.

Brubaker, Pamela K., Rebecca Todd Peters, and Laura A. Stivers, eds. *Justice in a Global Economy: Strategies for Home, Community, and World.* Louisville: Westminster John Knox, 2006.

Chopp, Rebecca S. *The Power to Speak: Feminism, Language, God*. New York: Crossroad, 1989.

Dawn, Marva J. *Reaching out Without Dumbing Down: A Theology of Worship for the Turn-of-the-Century Culture*. Grand Rapids: Eerdmans, 1995.

Dube, Musa. "Adinkra! Four Hearts Joined Together," 131–56 in *African Women, Religion, And Health: Essays In Honor Of Mercy Amba Ewudzi Oduyoye*, ed. Isabel Apawo Phiri, Sarojini Nadar, and Mercy Amba Oduyoye. Maryknoll, NY: Orbis Books, 2006.

Emerson, Michael O. and Christian Smith. *Divided By Faith: Evangelical Religion and the Problem of Race in America*. Oxford: Oxford University Press, 2000.

Farley, Margaret A. *Just Love: A Framework for Christian Sexual Ethics*. New York: Continuum International, 2006.

Geaves, Ron. *Key Words in Judaism*. Washington, DC: Georgetown University Press, 2007.

Geertz, Clifford. *The Interpretation of Cultures: Selected Essays*. New York: Basic Books, 1973.

González, Justo L. *Mañana: Christian Theology from a Hispanic Perspective*. Nashville: Abingdon Press, 1990.

Gottwald, Norman K. "Framing Biblical Interpretation at New York Theological Seminary: A Student Self-Inventory on Biblical Hermeneutics," 251–61 in *Reading from This Place*, vol. 1, *Social Location and Biblical Interpretation in the United States*, eds. Fernando F. Segovia and Mary Ann Tolbert. Minneapolis: Fortress Press, 1995.

Graff, Gerald and Cathy Birkenstein. *They Say / I Say: The Moves that Matter in Academic Writing*. New York: W. W. Norton & Co., 2010.

Hopkins, Dwight N. *Being Human: Race, Culture, and Religion*. Minneapolis: Fortress Press, 2005.

Jenkins, Philip. *The Next Christendom: The Coming of Global Christianity*. 3d ed. Oxford: Oxford University Press, 2011.

Lategan, Bernard C. "Hermeneutics," 149–54 in *The Anchor Bible Dictionary*, ed. David Noel Freedman. New York: Doubleday, 1992.

Lederach, John Paul. *The Little Book of Conflict Transformation*. Intercourse, PA: Good Books, 2003.

Marshall, Ellen Ott. *Christians in the Public Square: Faith that Transforms Politics*. Nashville: Abingdon, 2008.

McKim, Donald, ed. *How Karl Barth Changed My Mind*. Grand Rapids: Eerdmans, 1986.

Miller-McLemore, Mark. "Revaluing 'Self-Care' as a Practice of Ministry." *Journal of Religious Leadership* 10, no. 1 (2011): 109–34.

Oduyoye, Mercy Amba. "A Coming Home to Myself: The Childless Woman in the West African Space," 105–20 in *Liberating Eschatology: Essays in Honor of Letty Russell*, ed. Margaret A. Farley and Serene Jones. Louisville: Westminster John Knox, 1999.

———. "Be a Woman and Africa Will Be Strong," 35–53 in *Inheriting our Mothers' Gardens: Feminist Theology in Third World Perspective*, ed. Letty Russell et. al. Philadelphia: Westminster Press, 1988.

Patte, Daniel. *Ethics of Biblical Interpretation: A Reevaluation*. Louisville: Westminster John Knox, 1995.

Rawls, John. "Justice as Fairness." *The Philosophical Review* 67/2 (1958): 164–94.

Ricoeur, Paul. *Interpretation Theory: Discourse and the Surplus of Meaning*. Fort Worth: Texas Christian University Press, 1976.

Ruether, Rosemary Radford. *Sexism and God-Talk: Toward a Feminist Theology*. Boston: Beacon Press, 1983.

Russell, Letty M. *Household of Freedom: Authority in Feminist Theology*. The 1986 Annie Kinkead Warfield Lectures. Philadelphia: Westminster Press, 1987.

Saiving, Valerie. "The Human Situation: a Feminine View." *Journal of Religion* 40 (April 1960): 100–12.

Scalise, Charles J. *Hermeneutics as Theological Prolegomena: A Canonical Approach*. Studies in American Biblical Hermeneutics 8. Macon, GA: Mercer University Press, 1994.

Schüssler Fiorenza, Elisabeth. *Jesus and the Politics of Interpretation*. New York and London: Continuum, 2001.

Segovia, Fernando F. "Cultural Studies and Contemporary Biblical Criticism: Ideological Criticism as Mode of Discourse," 1–17 in *Reading from this Place*, vol. 2, *Social Location and Biblical Interpretation in Global Perspective*, ed. Fernando F. Segovia and Mary Ann Tolbert. Minneapolis: Fortress Press, 2000.

Shirky, Clay. *Here Comes Everybody: The Power of Organizing Without Organizations*. New York: Penguin, 2008.

Steinmetz, David C. "The Superiority of Pre-critical Exegesis," 26–38 in *The Theological Interpretation of Scripture: Classic and Contemporary Readings*, ed. Stephen E. Fowl. Malden, MA: Blackwell, 1997.

Tate, W. Randolph. *Biblical Interpretation: an Integrated Approach*. 3rd ed. Grand Rapids: Baker, 2011.

Tillich, Paul. *Systematic Theology*, Volume 1. Chicago: University of Chicago Press, 1967.

———. *The Courage to Be*. New Haven: Yale University Press, 1952.

Tracy, David. *Plurality and Ambiguity: Hermeneutics, Religion, Hope*. San Francisco: Harper & Row, 1987.

Van Til, Kent A. *Less Than Two Dollars a Day: A Christian View of World Poverty and the Free Market*. Grand Rapids: Eerdmans, 2007.

Weems, Renita J. "Re-reading for Liberation: African American Women and the Bible," 27–39 in *Voices From the Margin: Interpreting the Bible in the Third World*, ed. R. S. Sugirtharajah. Maryknoll, NY: Orbis Books, 2006.

Wimbush, Vincent L. "The Bible and African Americans: An Outline of an Interpretive History," 26–38 in *The Theological Interpretation of Scripture: Classic and Contemporary Readings*, ed. Stephen E. Fowl. Malden, MA: Blackwell, 1997.